HISTORIC GRAVES, PRIVATE BURIAL GROUNDS AND CEMETERIES

OF

KENT COUNTY, MARYLAND

Historical Society
of Kent County

HERITAGE BOOKS
2019

HERITAGE BOOKS

AN IMPRINT OF HERITAGE BOOKS, INC.

Books, CDs, and more—Worldwide

For our listing of thousands of titles see our website
at
www.HeritageBooks.com

Published 2019 by
HERITAGE BOOKS, INC.
Publishing Division
5810 Ruatan Street
Berwyn Heights, Md. 20740

International Standard Book Number
Paperbound: 978-1-58549-450-7

Historic Graves, Private Burial
Grounds and Cemeteries
of Kent County, Maryland

Compiled by a committee for the Historical Society
of Kent County. This Research Project was begun
and 1969 and completed in 1972.

Committee Members: Francis Lamb (chairman),
Joseph G. Stavely, Mrs. Joseph G. Stavely and
Ruby G. Doushkees. Assisted by Walker B. Lamb,
Elmer Lloyd, Mrs. Elmer Lloyd, Miss Helena Van-
Zant, Robert L. Usilton, Mrs. Simon W. Westcott,
and Robert Newman.

Historic Graves, Private Burial Grounds and Cemeteries of Kent County,
Maryland

Private Cemeteries

1. Mr. Wilbur Ross Hubbard's farm (The Wickes Family):
Sacred to the Memory of Colonel Joseph Wickes who was born September 2, 1788
and departed this life on January 14, 1864.
Sacred to the Memory of My Mother Mary Wickes relict of Joseph Wickes who
departed this life March 29, 1823 aged 59 years. (born 1764)
Sacred to the Memory of My Sister Sarah Wickes who departed this life on
August 26, 1844 aged 58 years. (born 1786)
Sacred to the Memory of My Father Joseph Wickes who departed this life on
August 16, 1822 aged 63 years. (born 1759)
Sacred to the Memory of Anna Maria Wickes wife of Joseph N. Wickes who
departed this life on April 2, 1864 aged 38 years. (born 1826)
B. Chambers Wickes who departed this life on 1st day of July A.D. 1854 in
the Thirty first year of his age. (born 1823)
Sacred to the Memory of Ezekiel Chambers Wickes who departed this life on
June 30, 1861 in the 30th year of his age. (born 1831)
Elizabeth C. Wickes relict of Col. Joseph Wickes who departed this life on
March 10th 1872 aged 73 years. (born 1799)
Several fieldstones also found in the Wickes Family Cemetery.

2. Graveyard where Eli Plummer and two of his wives are buried, no stones.
Green Point, Route 298.
Note by Francis L. Lamb, found in old Kent News newpaper and Lamb Family
Bible. Eli Plummer, Born 1776, Died May 9, 1844.
Achsah Lamb Plummer, Born Nov. 13, 1789, Died Nov. 17, 1823. Achsah Lamb
Birth and Death are in the John Brown Bible, which has belonged in the Lamb
Family since 1812, now in the possession of Francis L. Lamb of Chestertown,
Md. This is where John Cochran lives.

3. Farm where John Plummer now lives; graveyard is now gone; also old stone
with name of Frisby on it. Note: Mrs. Frances Stavely was born there, and
she remembers a stone with Frisby in the yard as a child.

4. Graveyard near Great Oak where Mr. Henry Demain built a house. Now a
colored club is build over part of the cemetery. Mrs. Emily Plummer Hudson
remembers as a child that one was there; her father and mother lived there
for some years.

5. Comegys Bight Farm, Quaker Neck: The home of Mrs. Louise Watson,
deceased. The Comegys, Brown and Jones Cemetery:
In Memory of Edward Comegys, Born April 12 1788, Died March 26, 1865.
Hiram Brown, Born Aug. 3, 1814, Died May 18, 1864.
Henrietta Nicholson, Dau. of Nathan & Nancy Hatcherson, Born July 1, 1819,
Died Feb. 10, 1896.
To the memory of my mother, Ann R. Merritt, Born Feb. 12, 1812, Died Oct 26,
1857.
Edward C. Brown, Born Feb. 10, 1810, Died Sept. 28, 1831.
Hiram Brown, Died June 7, 1848, Aged 68 (born 1780).
Mary, Consort of Hiram Brown, Born Sept. 1, 1786, Died Oct 5, 1825.
Susan B. Jones, Died Sept. 30, 1871 in the 3rd year of her age. (born 1868)

Harry C. Jones son of O. P. & M. E. Jones
Wm. U. Brown, Born June 12, 1789, Died Sept. 1, 1861.
Mary E. Jones 1812 - 1901
Oliver P. Jones, Born June 4, 1817, Died June 21, 1868.
Thomas F. Son of Cornelius C. & Lizzie T. Brown, Born Jan. 21, 1854, Died
Sept. 25, 1855.
Edward C. Brown, son of Cornelius C. & Lizzie T. Brown, Born July 2, 1855,
Died Sept. 15, 1855.
C. C. Brown, Born July 13, 1821, Died Apr. 21, 1865.
Lizzie T. Brown, Born June 30, 1829, Died July 23, 1903.
Thomas Trew, Beloved Son of Cornelius Comegys.
Elizabeth Thomas Brown, Born June 23, 1856, Died Jan. 14, 1903.
Mary Ida wife of Thomas T. Brown, born in Elmira, N. Y. on Dec. 5 1863, died
in Brooklyn, N. Y. on May 27, 1891.
Several fieldstones were found in the Comegys, Brown and Jones cemeteries.

6. White House Farm, 213N, near Kennedyville:
Here lieth the Body of Ebenezer Perkins who departed this life the 27th day
of August 1750 in the 34 year of his age. (born 1726)
    Life like a vain amusement, Flys a fable of a song
    By swift degrees nature dies, Nor can our joys be long
    Oh therefore learned the heavenly am. T(ime) improved the hours you have
    Then you will act the wiser part and live beyond the grave.
Three stones were found at the White House Farm.
Sacred to the memory of Mary Stuart wife of Doc. A. Stuart, who departed
this life Jan. 8, AD 1803 Age 39 years. (born 1764) "She was pious
friendly and humane Amiable in disposition and as a wife and Mother, most
affectionate and Soothing and endearing sensible and designed the last
breath hung of her soul were come Lord Jesus come quickly." God my redeemer
lives and often from the skys looks down and watches all my dust, till he
should see it rise.

7. Still Pond:
In Memory of Anna H. wife of Thomas Gale, Born June 23, 1778(9), Died March
22, 1819.
In Memory of Thomas Gale, Born March 14, 1762, Died Nov. 15, 1837.
In Memory of Mary, dau. of Thomas & A. Gale, Born April 14, 1807, Died April
8, 1854.
(12 fieldstones were also found.)
In Memory of William Gale, Born March 24, 1758, Died Aug. 27, 1817.
In Memory of Martha H. Gale wife of William Gale, Born Jan. 30th, 1764, Died
Apr. 25, 1805.
In Memory of Martha H. Gale wife of Colonel James Gale, Died 1857 Age 62.
(born 1795)
In Memory of Colonel James H. Gale, Died Aug. 6, 1808, Age 78 years (born
1730).

8. The Alms House Farm (Home of Mr. Walker B. Lamb):
Sacred to the Memory of Jo's & Mary Hynson the former aged about 45 years,
the latter aged about 30 years. Note: Joseph died 1802; his mother was a
Ringgold.

9. Tarbutton Farm near Shrewsbury.
Within this enclosure are the remains of the following named persons:

Colonel Edw'd Blay & wife of England.
William Blay, only son of Edward & wife and wife Issabella, daughter of
Colonel Pearce, with their issue: Rachel, Catherine, Issabella, Edward and
William.
Rachel Blay & Peregrine* Brown, of England, her husband and their son
Peregrine, her second husband, Aquilla Pearce* and their daughter Martha.
Catherine & John Tilden and their children Issabella & Richard Wethered of
London, her husband, and their children, William, John, Samuel & John. (Wm.
excepted – this inscription & the enclosure done by the direction of John
Wethered who died on the 21st of Feb. 1822. In the 77 year of his age.
Edward Blay Doner of this Graveyard 1709. This stone was removed from
"Blay's Range" by Mr. L. Wethered Barroll and Mr. James Henry Groves to
Shrewsbury Church in 1958.

* The inscribed names of the husbands of Rachel Blay are in error.
Peregrine Brown should read John Brown and Aquilla Pearce should read
Aquilla Paca.

10. On Mary Morris Road:
Sacred to the Memory of P. Wroth, M. D., Born April 7, 1786, Died Jun 13,
1879.
In Memory of Margaret S. dau. of Samuel & Eliza Nicols, Born March 31, 1802,
married Dr. P. Wroth June 19 1827, Died Dec. 13, 1836.
In Memory of Martha P. Wroth dau. of John & Milcah Page, Born Aug. 5, 1779,
Married Dr. P. Wroth Aug. 27, 1807, Died Sept. 23, 1826.
Mary Cecilia Wroth, Born July 19, 1808, Died July 30, Age 20 days.
Sacred to the Memory of Eugenia Marie wife of Edward T. Wroth and dau. of
Peregrine & Martha P. Wroth, Born Feb. 26, 1817, Died Sept. 30, 1861.
You have been so beloved none ever deserved it more Blessed are the dead who
die in the Lord.

11. Green Point:
In Memory of Sarah wife of Samuel Groom Kennard, Born March 6, 1791, Died
July 7, 1847.
    My Mothers face no more I see
        She dwells Oh Lord in heaven with thee
    Oh that she would look down
        And Smile upon her orphan.
In Memory of Mary Kennard.

12. Brice's Mill Road (Thompson Farm):
Perkins (This is part of the same Perkins family at Brice's Mill, that
lived at the White House Farm.)
Eliza Perkins daughter of Daniel & Susannah Perkins, Born June 15, 1796,
Died March 18, 1857 (age almost 61).
In Memory of Anna Perkins daughter of Daniel & Susannah Perkins who departed
this life on June 9, 1861 in the 67th year of her age. An affectionate
daughter a devoted sister and a faithful friend. (born 1794)
Caroline Perkins, Born Oct. 28, 1804, Died Jun 22, 1882 (age 78). A true
woman
Daniel Perkins son of Daniel & Susannah Perkins Died April 1840, Age 10
(born 1830).
Sarah Perkins, Born March 14, 1792, Died Jan. 18, 1855.
Daniel Perkins, Died April, 1811, Age 17 (born 1794).

Susannah Perkins, Died Dec. 1821, Aged 56 (born 1765).
James A. Perkins, Born July 27, 1851, Died December 1, 1852. A. Gadis
Bahti.
Ebenezer Perkins son of J. A. & M. E. P., Born March 1861, Died May 7, 1863.
In Memory of Elizabeth Wickes, Died May 1850, aged 78 (born 1772).

13. Clarks Conveniency at Norman Grieb Farm (Quaker Neck):
Edward Wilkens, Died May 5, 1814 in the 45 year of his age. A. Gaddis,
Balto.
(Denes Clark) 7 fieldstones mark 7 graves.

14. Trew Family Cemetery at "Providence Plantation:"
Thomas W. Trew, Born 7 Mo. 20th, 1794, Died 12 mo. 6th 1859. Footstone: TWT
Elizabeth Trew wife of T. W. Trew, Born 4th mo. 27th, 1810, Died 7th mo.
11th, 1876. Footstone: E. T.
In Memory of Bartus Trew, Born on the 1st day of the 1st mo. 1780, Died on
the 20th day of the 10th mo. 1836. Footstone: B. T.
William Trew, son of william & Mary Trew, Born 6th mo. 8 day 1774, Died 4th
mo. 8 day 1802. Footstone: W. T.
Mary Trew daughter of William & Mary Trew, Born 2nd mo. 1, 1789, Died 3rd
mo. 9, 1842. Footstone: M. T.
William Trew, Born 12 mo. 19, 1751, Died 10 mo. 15, 1815. Footstone: W. T.
Mary Trew wife of William Trew, Born 4 mo. 2, 1755, Died 2 mo. 13, 1813.
Footstone: M. T.
Mary Trew daughter of William & Mary Trew, Born 3 mo. 30, 1782, Died 9 mo.
1, 1785.
Deborah Trew daughter of Bartus & Mary Trew, Born 8th, mo. 31, 1799, Died
10th mo. 17, 1876. Footstone: D. T.
Ann Rebecca daughter of Bartus & Sallie S. Trew, Born the 21st of the 4th
mo. 1828, Died on 4th of the 11th mo. 1831. Footstone: A. R. T.
Elizabeth S. Trew daughter of Bartus & Sarah S. Trew, Born 12 mo. 12, 1830,
Died 1 mo. 25, 1868, Footstone: E. S. T.
Mary E. Trew, born 2 mo. 26th, Died 7 mo. 18th, 1818. Footstone: M. E. T.
Sally A. Trew, Born 11 mo. 25, 1832, Died 5 mo. 22nd, 1834. Footstone: S.
A. T.
Philip E. Trew, Born June 8, 1844, Died Aug. 2, 1904. Footstone: P. E. T.
Thomas B. Trew son of Thomas W. & Elizabeth Trew, Jan. 1, 1838, Jan. 1,
1913, a devoted husband.
A. Trew Born 1860, Died 1860
Infant of Thomas W. & Elizabeth Trew
Infant of Jno. C. & Sallie G. Ruth Born Nov. 1847.
Sarah S. wife of Edward Brown, Born Nov. 13, 1803, Died Apr. 4, 1874.
Sarah E. daughter of William & Emoline Simmons, June 30, 1833, March 31,
1912.
Jacob Knotts Born 8 mo. 1802, Died 6 mo. 16, 1868. Footstone: J. K.
In Memory of Sarah wife of Thomas B. Hamilton, Died Aug. 4, 1870, 73 year of
her age, Beloved sleep, He girdle his beloveth sleep.
In Memory of Thomas D. Hamilton who died March 20, 1857 in the 56th year of
his age. Also of Joshua Thomas infant son of Thomas & Sarah Hamilton who
died Sept. 26, 1857 aged 4 months & 20 days.
In Memory of Susannah Hamilton who died May 30, 1841 age 7 years.
Sacred to the Memory of Jas. T. Wilkins, Born Feb. 10, 1810, Died Apr. 16,
1882, age 72 years 2 months & 6 days. Many are the affication of the
righteous, but the Lord delivers him out of them all.

W. George son of M. G. & M. A. Trew, Born Nov. 24, 1865, Died Feb. 24, 1868.
Footstone: W. G. T.

15. Near Still Pond (between Turner's Creek and Lloyd Creek):
Placque: This farm known as Luck was surveyed for James Hepbron or Hepburn
in 1683 and remained in the family until 1906 when sold to Tilden Cooper.
Only portions of the inscription on the fieldstone are readable:
    The 29 ....Th OMAS SH ... THE

Hepbroun Monument at Mr. & Mrs. William Cooper's Farm.
Fieldstone is in Monument. Inscription partially readable:
HAE
... Chaatheer
Hepbroun
Thomas Hepbroun   .... Jacob   Small Stone

Plaque: To James Hepburn And descendants buried here from 1683 - 1830
Fieldstone: Thomas Hepb...   May the 18 ...
Margaret Hepbourn

16. Ringgold Cemetery, Chestertown, behind the Kent & Queen Anne's
Hospital, formerly the property of Byford Court and owned by Mr. and Mrs.
Morris K. Barroll:
This stone designates the spot where lies the Sacred remains of George W.
Ringgold who died in the 55 year of his age in full assurance of a blissfull
immortality beyond the grave leaving a wife and child to mourn their
irreparable loss.
In Memory of Hannah wife of William Smith who died June 21, 1851 (born 1779)
in the 72nd year of her age.
    Her end was peace and now the pain of life is past
    All her warfare now is o'er
    Death and Hell are behind us are cast
    Grief and suffering are no more
In Memory of John Fletcher Ringgold, Born February 1st. 1822, Died January
25, 1855 in the 33rd year of his age. He was a devoted husband and an
affectionate father. A dutiful son. He died with the full assurance of a
blissfull immortality. A short time before his death, he exclaimed, I am
now ready to be offered as the time of my departure is at hand. I have
fought a good fight, I have lived a good life, I have sped my course, I have
kept the faith.
In Memory of Edward Ringgold, Died Dec. 10, 1851 in the 80th year of his age
(born 1771).
In Memory of Rebecca Consort of Edward Ringgold, Died Sept. 20th 1857 In the
81st year of her age (born 1776). Her end was peace.
    Servant of God. Well done thy Glorious warfare's past
    The battle's fought, the race is won and thou are Crowned at last
Footstone: E. S. or E. B.
My Brother Charles Tilden, Son of Dr. Wm. Blay & Mary B. He died Nov. 18,
(year broken off), Aged 50 years.
In Memory of E. Lane wife of Charles Tilden and daughter of the late Edw.
Ringgold who died Oct. 3, 1856, aged 39 years. (Born 1817). Footstone:
E. L. T.

In Memory of William Edward only son of Geo. W. & Louisa Ringgold who changed mortality for life Febry 1, 1852, aged 7 years 2 months and 2 days (Born Dec. 31, 1843.

17. Near Galena:
Pennington Cemetery which no longer exists, but which is remembered by Miss Helena VanZant, whose grandparents, John Henry & Susan A. Pennington Jarvis lived on the Pennington Farm for 30 years, from 1878 to 1908. This farm is now owned by Mr. & Mrs. Dorsey Owens.

18. Above Galena, on Route 290:
My Husband George H. Brice, Died Feb. 21, 1874 in 31st year of his age.
Footstone: G. H. B.
   Here lies a kind husband father dear,
   His god's will he should be here.
   We hope our loss will be his gain,
   In hoping heaven he may obtain.
Emma S. Brice Sept. 5, 1858, July 13, 1921.
My Dutiful Son William Nathaniel son of William A. and Mary Ann Brice, Died July 23 1869 aged 31 years 7 mo. 14 days (born Dec. 9 1838)
Sally Ann Elizabeth Brice, Died Feb 15th, 1814, Age 1 year, 15 days (Born Jan. 31, 1813). Footstone: S. A. E. B.
James Richard Brice , Died Sept. 12th 1823, 1 year 11 mo. (born Nov 12 1821)
In Memory of James Brice who departed this life May 28, 1825 aged 45 years 4 months and 20 days (born Jan. 8, 1789)
William A. Brice, Born Oct 27, 1810, Died Sept. 21, 1873. Blessed are the Dead who die in the name of the Lord
Mary A. Brice Footstone: M. A. B.
Born Dec 8 1818, Died Dec 24 1882.
Blessed are the Dead who die in the Lord

19. Near Georgetown, at Colchester Farm, west of Georgetown, above Galena:
To the Memory of Mr. & Mrs. James Pearce and of their eldest son of James Pearce, Esqr. This Tribute of Filial Sisterly affection is Erected by their last Surviving Daughter & Sister. Here also are deposited the Remains of Mrs. Julia Pearce, the sister and chosen friend of her heart. 1847   A. Gaddis, Maker, Balt.
Stones erected for the following: Anna Pearce; Mrs. Jas. Pearce; Mrs. Julia Pearce; Mrs. Hyson; Elizabeth Pearce; Mrs. James Pearce
Monument: Within this enclosure interred the remains of her two parental Aunts Two Elder Sisters, Mrs. Hyson (Hynson) Misses Isabella, Elizabeth & Anne Pearce - 1847

20. Caulk's Field Farm, on Tulip Forest Farm, below Fairlee:
There are about 12 or more graves, no stones. This could be the gravesite of British soldiers killed in the War of 1812. According to Percy Granger Skirven, "At Caulk's Field the British lost 9 men killed and 1 midshipman, 9 men wounded, 6 died within a few hours."

21. Also on Tulip Forest Farm:
Sacred to the memory of Samuel Eccleston who departed this life October 29th, 1802 much Lamented

Ann Bowers Eccleston Born Jan 22, 1773, Died July 14, 1798. He giveth His
beloveth Sleep. Fieldstone marked A. E.
Sacred to the memory of Mrs. Sarah Bowers wife of Major James Bowers, Died
July 15th, 1818, Aged 49 years 9 months and 4 days. (born Nov. 11, 1768)
Owned by Mr. C. Van Stohl of Rotterdam, Holland, which is Caulk's Field
Farm, Tulip Forrest Farm of the Haddaway Farm.

22. Memorials at Worton Manor or Worton Point, Andelot Farm. The Andelot
Farm owned in 1971 by Lammot duPont Copeland. At a point of land near the
once called Maxwell home on Worton Creek and an inlet, Timm's Creek; now a
bordering of woods by the creek, myrtle growing over an open plot, some
sunken places and one broken stone in three pieces.
John Bordley died Dec. 21, 1815 aged 51 (born 1764).
Catherine Bordley Died January 26, 1838 aged 62 (born 1776)
Catherine Stark died 1818 aged 70 (born 1748)
Benjamin Stark Born Nov. 18,   Died Jan. 18,
Minta   Faithful and valiant servant of the Barroll Family died November 15,
1836 aged 60.   Nearby is a large heavy iron fenced plot about 6 x 8 feet,
one stone (buried) and a footstone.
In memory of Benjamin Starck, Born Nov. 9, 1814, Died Jan'y 18, 1854.

23. Langcroft Farm, Broad Neck, owned by Mrs. Georgia Bloecher and Mrs.
Alice B. Nelson:
Rosamond Maslin Born 10th of the 8th month 1789, Died 22nd d. of 1st month
1854 Aged 64 years 5 months & 12 days.
Susan J. Maslin died May 17, 1863, Aged 26 years.
Anna Eliza B. Maslin departed this life May 5th 1862, Aged 63 years
Note on gravestones at Langcroft Farm: Rosamond Lamb, dau. of George &
Sarah Briscoe Lamb, Married Jacob Maslin, son of Thomas III and Martha Glenn
Maslin and grandson of Thomas II and Mary Ann Lamb Maslin. Susan Jemima
Maslin, dau. of John A. & Elizabeth Blackiston Maslin, was born 1838,
granddaughter of James & Hannah Maslin, great granddaughter of Thomas II &
Mary Ann Lamb Maslin. Anna Eliza Baker, dau. of Thomas & Margaret Baker,
was born Dec. 12, 1799, Married, Edwin World Maslin, son of Francis &
Rebecca Thomas Ferrill Maslin, grandson of Thomas II & Mary Ann Lamb Maslin.

Note: Michael Miller Maslin, son of Thomas II & Martha Glenn Maslin, was
born in 1788, died in Broad Neck, Kent Co., Md. on Feb. 8, 1852. His death
was in Old Kent News, at the Kent County New's office in Chestertown, Md.
Thomas I & Jane Britain (married in England)
Thomas Maslin II & Mary Ann Lamb, married in Kent Co., Md.
Thomas Maslin III & Martha Glenn, married in Kent Co., Md.
Michael Miller Maslin & Elizabeth Sarah Moieler, married in York, Pa.
Caroline Maslin & Robert Ewing, married in Phila., Pa.
Caroline Maslin Ewing & John Vernon Bouvier, married in Phila., Pa.
John Vernon Bouvier II and Maude Frances Sargeant, married in New York
John Vernon Bouvier III & Janet Lee, married in New York.
Jacqueline Lee Bouvier & John F. Kennedy, married in Mass.

24. Trumpington Farm, Eastern Neck Road, home of Mr. & Mrs. Ernest Willson.
Mrs. Willson was formerly Miss Mary Ringgold.
D. C. Wilson born Oct. 21st 1828, died March 5th 1876. Footstone: D. C. W.
Fieldstone: S. H.   Fieldstone: C. B. W.
10 fieldstones

Mary A. wife of Tho. Willson, died June 4, 1847, aged 32. Footstone: M. A. W.

Thomas Willson son of Tho. S. B. Willson & Mary Hall, Born September 28, 1778, Died October 28th, 1859.

Anna M. wife of Tho. Wilson, Died April 28th 1823, aged 37 years.

Sarah daughter of Matthew & Sarah Tilghman, Wife of Francis G. Hall, Born March 28, 1788, Died September 29, 1812.

Matthew son of Edward & Julian Tilghman, Born June 5th, 1760 and Died 9th Feb. 1801. Footstone: M. T.

Sarah daughter of Thomas & Margaret Smyth and wife of Matthew Tilghman, Born 8th June 1767 and Died 8th July 1791. Footstone: S. T.

Thos. Smyth died March 19th, 1813, aged 90 years less 14 days. Footstone: T. S.

25. William's Venture, Humphrey's Point Farm owned by Mrs. Berthold Bothe, Rock Hall, Md.:
Sacred to the memory of Ann Humphrey consort of John Humphrey, M. D. Kent county who departed this life 30th   1820. (in the) 30th year of her age.
Lay not up treasures on earth where moth and rust collect, But rather lay up treasures in heaven where moth and rust doth not collect.

26. Vickers Farm, now owned by Mr. & Mrs. Henry W. Johnstone in Quaker Neck:
In memory of Benjamin Vickers who was born on the 18th of November 1761 and died on 29th of May, 1835.

27. Property owned by Mrs. Elmer Gustafson in Quaker Neck. This private cemetery was bulldozed about 19 years ago and is now being tilled over.
William Lamb, Jr. son of William & Rebekah Pearce Lamb was born March 30, 1824 and died December 25, 1860.

28. Kemp's Beginning, now Airy Hill Farm, on Airy Hill Road.
Sacred to the memory of Dr. George W. Thomas who was born January 8th A. D. 1781 and departed this life March 4th A. D. 1842.
Sacred to the memory of Mary S. Thomas Relict of Dr. Geo. W. Thomas Who departed this life March 25 A. D. 1850 aged 70 years.
Note: Mary S. Thomas, was formerly Mary S. Leatherbury.

29. Pippin Hill Farm, now Alfalfa Dell Farm, on Route 20, owned by Mr. & Mrs. G. Robert Moffett, Sr.
Milcha, wife of Richard W. Pippin died July 31, 1868 aged about 65 years (born 1803). Footstone: M. P.

30. Stephney Manor Home of Mr. & Mrs. Arthur Lusby, Sr.
Sacred to the memory of a Beloved Husband Joseph N. Gordon, Died April 28th, 1848, Age 73 years (born 1775). Blessed are they who die in the Lord"
Caroline A. Gordon died Febry. 22, 1845, Age 1 yr. & 6 mons (born Aug. 1843). Heaven has recalled its own.
Thos. W. Gemmell Died Nov. 1847, Aged 2 (born 1845). He gives and when he takes away He takes but what he gave.

Stephney Manor

Dr. Joseph Nicholson Gordon was the son of Charles Gordon and Elizabeth Nicholson, who was the daughter of Col. Joseph Nicholson, of Chestertown. Dr. Gordon married Mary Frisby of "Fairlee." She was the daughter of Ann Wilmer and James Frisby. Ann was the daughter of William Wilmer.

Dr. Joseph N. Gordon was High Sheriff of Kent County and Clerk of Circuit Court of Kent County 1827-48. (ancestors and relatives having held this office, including his own term, and that of his son James Frisby Gordon, for 106 years.

He was surgeon of the 21st Maryland Regiment during the second war with England, 1812-1814. The English in 1814 sent a powerful expedition to the Chesapeake and carried fire and sword throughout the shore. They burnt Washington, attacked Baltimore and burnt towns and plantations on the Eastern Shore. On August 21st, 1814, Sir Peter Parker, commanding the frigate Memelaus, landed and burnt Fairlee, the ancestral home of Dr. Gordon's wife, Mary Frisby Gordon.

Learning that a small force of 174 men of the 21st Regiment was encamped nearby, he decided to surprise them. He landed 250 men for this purpose. It was a brillian moonlight night and Lt. Col. Philip Reed of the 21st Regiment soon learned of their advance. The action took place at Caulk's Field and was a spirited affair. Sir Peter Parker was mortally wounded and the British soon drew off.

Dr. Gordon was a farmer and stock raiser. In 1820 when Gen. Lafayette was his guest at Stephney, he won a silver cup for showing the best jack at a mule fair. Gen. Lafayette presented the trophy.

A deed of Lemuel Wilmer pertaining to the sale of the Stephney estate to Mary Frisby Gordon, Lemuel's cousin and wife of Dr. Gordon for the sum of $983 was dated July 1822.

Another deed records the sale of the place in 1858 by James Frisby Gordon, to his cousin, James Ricaud for $12,000, reserving the family graveyard to himself and his heirs in the garden, as now enclosed, to be used as a burial ground exclusively.

31. Armstrong Cemetery, former home of Mr. & Mrs. William Armstrong, now owned by Mr. & Mrs. William Briscoe, in Galena, Md.:
Wm. M. Armstrong/Sarah M. Armstrong.
John M. Armstrong His first wife Aramenta Johnson/Children - W. Joshua/J. Medford/S. Adelia/Araminta E. J./William
His second wife E. E. A. W. Johnson/Children - Elizabeth A. W./A. Louisa

Copied from Kent Shoreman by Mrs. Mary Jane Kaehn:
"RED GABLES NOW BUTTONWOOD - Present owners of this fine old home are Mr. & Mrs. William Briscoe. It was built in 1796 by William Armstrong, great great grandfather of Mrs. Briscoe. The first owner of this property comprising some 125 acres was William Armstrong, Sr. Mr. Armstrong was born in Newark, Delaware. He served in the War of 1812. Mrs. Briscoe's grandfather also resided in the house. He was the Rev. Allison Palmer Prettyman, a Methodist minister. Mrs. Briscoe was born and raised in this house by the Rev. & Mrs. Prettyman."

32. Dodd Farm, Flat Lane Road near Washington Park. About 15 fieldstones.

33. Glen More Farm, owned by Mrs. Simon Westcott and the late Mrs. Charles Schaeffer, west of Kennedyville on Turner's Creek Road, west side. About 15 fieldstones in cemetery.

34. Knock's Folly Farm, Turner's Creek. Cemetery has about 10 fieldstones and 6 granite stones uncut. Members of Redgrave, Stavely and Webb families are buried here.
In memory of William D. Webb who departed this life August 18th, 1844 aged 4 years. Suffer little children to come unto me. Forbid them not for such is the kingdom of heaven. Footstone: W. D. W.
In memory of Virginia Webb who departed this life Oct. 18, 1845 aged 3 years and 2 months. The Lord God hath taken away, Blessed be the name of the Lord.

35. Old Field Point Farm, now part of Starkey Farms, Inc., near Galena. Wilson, Rasin, Ringold & Heighe.
William George Wilson, who departed this life December 16, 1845, aged 28 yrs., 7 months, 5 days (born May 11, 1817).
In memory of Robert Wilson, son of Robert and Eliza Who departed this life 4th Nov. 1816 aged 14 months and 3 days (born Sept. 1, 1815). Footstone: R. W. 1816
James M. Rasin February 6, 1811 - February 11, 1880
In memory of Martha R. daughter of William and Mary R. Ringgold born Nov. 27, 1823, died Dec. 3, 1854. Footstone: M. R. R.
In memory of Augusta Lavenia daughter of H. H. and Anna Rasin who departed this life March 8, 1851 aged 13 months 8 days (born Feb. 1850).
Phoebe Wilson only daughter of Robert and Mary R. Rasin died in Q. Ann's Co. Oct. 13, 1842, aged 7 years 7 months 18 days (born Feb. 25, 1835).
To our Mother Mary R. Rasin consort of Robert M. Rasin Born Feb'y 22, 1802, departed this life Nov. 15, 1860.
Anna Williamina Wilson daughter of George William & Anna Wilson, departed this life Aug. 31, 1841 aged 20 (born 1821).
In memory of Laura Jane Heighe daughter of James and Susan E. Heighe who departed this life June 9, 1842 aged 17 months 24 days (born Jan. 13, 1841). Footstone: L. J. H.
Georgianna Louisa daughter of James and Susan E. Heighe departed this life March 29, 1834, aged one year 6 months (born Sept. 29, 1832)
In Memory of Wilbert Wilson son of Robert & Mary Wilson who departed this life May 28th, 1822 aged 4 months and 22 days.
>Dearest darling boy thy pains are ore
>Thy little hart shall ache no more
>A mother watched your fading smile
>And all her fears and cares beguile
>But God called thee soon away
>When he commends we must obey.

Also 25 fieldstones were found in this cemetery at Old Field Point Farm. Also were found at Starkey Farms in a gravel pit, 4 graves, some of which the skull and other bones were laying at the bottom of the pit, the others were with leg bones exposed. About 42 or more graves in this cemetery.

In memory of Margaret Wilson daughter of Robert & Eliza who departed this life 17th Sept. 1813, Aged 1 year, 13 days (born Sept. 4, 1812). Footstone: M. W. 1813

In memory of George William Wilson who departed this life December 30th 1841 aged 58 years (born 1783).
In memory of Edwin Wilson son of Robert & Eliza who departed this life on the 5th of Aug. 1814 aged 7 months & 21 days.
In memory of Meliscent Rogers who departed this life the 8 ... 1800. Footstone: M. R.
In memory of Eliza Wilson wife of Robert Wilson who departed this life May 2nd 1818 aged 26 years 4 months 5 days (born may 28, 1792)
This stone is erected to the memory of Robert Wilson who departed this life May 8th, 1822 aged 41 years 3 months and 26 days. The execellent virtues of this much lamented man are undelibly engraven on the hearts of his friends. He has left and gone to rest among the saints whom god has blest. (born Jan. 12, 1781)

36. Bachelor Hope Farm, Quaker Neck, below Cliff City, owned by Mr. & Mrs. Robert Hewes, II.
Register Cemetery (Stones are backs of barn):
William Register died Dec. 7th, 1817, aged 9 years 1 day. Footstone: w. R.
John K. Register died June 14th 1845, age 9 months & 23 d's.
Mary R. Register died October 14, 1835, age 5 mos. & 22 d.
Note: there is a cemetery on right side of the house but no stones are there.

37. Tilghman Farm, now Fair Hope Farm, Quaker Neck.
Cemetery in the boxwood garden in the rear of the house. Mrs. Stokes' ashes were buried there in 1969. Francis Lamb recalls his grandmother, who lived there on the place, as saying his great grandfather, William Lamb, would walk out early in the morning, and view the graves. Apparently his first two wives, Rebekah Pearce and Catherine Caroline Jones, are among the boxwood.

38. St. Clements Church Farm, east of Massey. The Rev. Ernest Richards outside of Massey, Md. Stephen Boyer gave this farm to St. Clements Church. Hurlock Cemetery:
Mary R. wife of Samuel Hurlock died Oct. 19, 1866 aged 35 years 10 mos. and 27 days. She made her home happy.
Samuel B. son of Samuel & Mary R. Hurlock died June 26, 1864 aged 3 years and 6 months.
Ernest S. son of Samuel and Mary R. Hurlock died Aug. 9, 1858 aged 8 mos. & 6 days.
Ernest M. son of Samuel & Mary R. Hurlock died Aug. 14, 1854 aged 1 year and 22 ds. Footstone: D. M. H.
David Alven son of W. C. & Sallie G. Footstone: D. A. T.

39. Cacy, Osborne, Boyer, Cemetery near Massey, owned by Mr. Gemberling.
In memory of Stephen P. Cacy died April 13th, 1851, aged 18 yrs., 3 mos. & 18 dys.
        In life beloved, now die at rest
        And God always takes those he loves best. Footstone: S. P. C.
Elizabeth A. Cacy wife of William Cacy died Oct. 2, 1888 in the 79th year of her age. Born 1809. Footstone: E. A. C.
Father – At Rest   John Evans Cacy Jan. 27, 1810, March 1, 1860.
His wife – Anna Maria Osborne Dec. 11, 1814, July 25 1880
John Evans, Jr. Aug. 25, 1842, Nov. 6 1845

Anna Cephelia Nov. 6, 1845, March 25, 1849
Children of John Evans and Anna Maria Osborne Cacy
W. Finley Collins Oct. 27, 1863, Dec. 11, 1918
William Cacy born Sept. 14, 1812, died Jan. 27th, 1892. Footstone: W. C.
Julia Evans Apr. 21, 1848, Nov. 28, 1930
Charles Osborne Cacy son of John Evans and Anna Maria Osborne Cacy May 9,
1850, Sept. 21, 1919
Footstones: A. C. C.; A. M. O. C.; J. E. C.; J. E. C.; C. O. C.
Agnes infant daughter of William and Kate Boyer died Aug. 4, 1866 aged 5
mos. and 9 ds. Footstone: A. B
William Evans son of William E. & Marcia S. Cacy Born June 19, 1906, Died
Aug. 6, 1907. Footstone: W. E. C.
John Evans son of William T. & Mollie Cacy died Feb. 18, 1851 aged 5 years,
3 mos. and 18 das. Footstone: J. E. C.
Stephen B. infant son of William E. & Mollie Cacy died June 3rd. 1868 aged 1
mo. and 9 das.
Vault - Sacred to the memory of Richard T. Boyer who died April 20th, 1857
in the 40th year of his age.
   Angel wings have borne his spirit to a purer land above
   Where the blest forever inherit All the Father's holy love.
Sophia wife of Richard T. Boyer died Sept. 12, 1860 in the 28th year of her
age.
Stephen Boyer died Feb. 21, 1838 aged 61 years 4 mos. 18 das.
Maria wife of Stephen Boyer died Dec. 21, 1854 aged 54 yr. 8 mo. and 20
days.
In memory of Urie Irving Boyer departed this life Jan. 30, 1855 aged 39
years 2 mos. and 19 days. In the midst of life we are in death.
William E. Cacy born May 10, 1888 died april 22, 1925
Husband William Boyer died Sept. 14, 1885 aged 54 years. Resting till their
resurrection morn.
Catherine J. wife of William Boyer died April 27th, 1871 aged 34 years.
Maria A. Boyer born January 15, 1825, died Jun 3, 1899
Mary Osborne wife of William Evans Cacy born March 2, 1840, died Dec. 21,
1912
At Rest   Footstone: M. O. C.
Stephen Boyer born March 31, 1828, died April 12, 1904
Agnes wife of Stephen Boyer died June 1, 1902, aged 76 years.
Brother Stephen Boyer August 4, 1888, February 7, 1904.

40. Hendrickson Farm, near Millington, now the Anderson Farm, owned by Mr.
& Mrs. Edward Anderson.
Col. Elijah E. Massey died Jan. 23, 1881, aged 66 years 6 mos. and 20 d.
(born July 3, 1814)
Mary E. wife of Elijah E. Massey died Jan. 29, 1859 in the 44 year of her
age (born 1805).
Mary E. daughter of E. E. & M. E. Massey died Sept. 17, 1864 in the 19th
year of her life (born 1845). Footstone: R. H. M.
Several fieldstones.
Eleanore P. daughter of E. E. & M. E. Massey died Aug. 24, 1845 in the 2nd
year of her age.
Charles A. son of E. E. & M. E. Massey died Sept. 24, 1835 in the second
year of his age.
Thomas J. son of E. E. & M. E. Massey died Sept. 4, 1843 age 3 years.

Charles F. son of E. E. & M. E. Massey died May 11th 1843 in the 2nd year of his age.
Charles K. son of W. H. & E. L. Neale born March 27, 1862, died April 20th 1877.
Willard C. son of W. H. & Eliza L. Neal died July 13, 1864, age 2 mos. 26 days.
Edgar H. son of W. H. & Eliza L. Neal died Sept. 13, 1870 age 1 year 11 months.
In memory of Eliza Neal July 15th, 1827, April 2, 1898
Henrietta A. daughter of E. E. & M. E. Massey died April 19th, 1853 in the 8th year of her age.
My darling son Robert H. Massey died December 25th, 1876 age 17 years 9 mos. and 27 da's.

> Past his suffering, Past his pain
> Ceased to weep, for tears are vain.
> Calm the tumult of the breast.
> He who suffered, is at rest
> Asleep in Jesus.

41. Quaker Cemetery at Millington, Md., Head of Chester:
Mary E. Edwards died Oct. 31, 1887, aged 21 years, 3 mos. & 12 das. (born July 19, 1866). Weep not she is not alive but sleepth.
Eliza wife of Arthur Sudler died Aug. 15, 1892, aged 85 years (born 1807). Gone but not forgotten.
Henrietta Evens Born Apirl 17, 1790, died May 6, 1855.
Florence C. Vansant died Sept. 22, 1808 aged 3 mos. and 20 da's. (born June 2, 1808)
Emma L. daughter of Benj. P. Wallers 9 mos. (note the stone was broken in half)
Fence around plot — John Nicholas son of Andrew A. & Ada D. Vansant born Dec. 24, 1899, died Aug. 17, 1901.
Meet me in Heaven
Mary Irene Lott born November 8th, 1869, died November 7th, 1882.

> Pa and Ma I must leave you all alone
> But my blessed Savior calls me to a heavenly home.

Mary H. Vansant Born 6 mos's, 22 da's 1817, Died 12 mo's 18 da's 1847.
Ada M. daughter of Nicholas and R. Vansant Died Mch. 23, 1879, Aged 25 ys, 11 mo's 15 days. Footstone: A. M. V.
J. Margaret Vansant died April
These are fenced in an enclosure.
John Nicholas son of Andrew W. and Ada G. Vansant Born Dec. 24 1899, Died Aug. 17, 1901.
Harry C. Vansant Born Sept. 20, 1880, Died Mary 29, 1906. Footstone: Brother
Emily A. Vansant Born Dec. 13, 1842, Died March 18, 1911
John N. Vansant Born Sept. 26, 1840, Died May 16, 1906.
Nicholas A. son of John N. and Emily A. Vansant Died Jan. 11, 1871, Age 1 yr. 2 mo's 5 days.
Nicholas C. son of John N. and Emily A. Vansant Died April 24, 1875, Age 3 yrs. 2 mo's 5 da's
Henrietta Evans Born April 17, 1790, Died May 6, 1811. Footstone: H. E.
Guilalma M. wife of James D. Edwards Died Feb. 11, 1873, 49th year of her age.

James B. son of J. A. and G. M. Edwards Died July 30, 1856, Age 10 yrs and 7 mo's.
William T. son of J. A. and G. M. Edwards Died Apr. 11, 1857 age 1 year
Susie E. daughter of J. A. and G. M. Edwards died May 10, 1860, Age 2 yrs. 7 mo's.
Sallie E. daughter of J. A. and G. M. Edwards Died Nov. 28, 1853 age 1 year 6 mos.
   No more I look for thee on earth A world of grief and pain
   But yet I know my darling baby I will see the again.
2 fieldstones
Emma L. died 1873
Other fieldstones and foot stones:
B. G.; B. O.; G. E.; B. L. B.; M.; J. M. B.; L. V.

42. Beck-Lyzer Cemetery on the Knolls on Smithville-St. James Church Road:
In memory of Mary Jane wife of James Beck of Geo. who was born Dec. 1, 1811 and died Aug. 18, 1844.
Sacred to the memory of Mary Beck died Oct 29, 1882 aged 84 years. Blessed are the pure in heart for theirs is the kingdom of heaven.
In Memory of Catherine E. wife of Capt. B. H. Stark born June 4th, 1809, died May 27, 1854. Footstone: C. E. S.

Beck Cemetery on Mr. Whitelaw's farm:
John son of Michael and Maria Lyzer died Oct. 8, 1847 aged 30 yrs. 9 mos. 22 das. Born Dec. 16, 1817.
Anne Maria daughter of Michael and Maria Lyzer died July 6, 1842 aged 21 years (born 1821).
One time a number of markers and one grave had a marker of a slave and the name.

43. Scone Cemetery - Part of Worton Manor, owned by Mr. & Mrs. Milton Myers (Mier)
In memory of Rachel K. consort of Arthur A. Scone died May 21, 1815 aged 25 years, 7 mos. 25 das. Footstone: R. K. S.
   I sought the Lord and he heard me; yea, he delivered me out of all my fears. Thanks be to God, who giveth us the victory through our Lord Jesus Christ.
Fieldstone marked A. S. 1811
Several unmarked fieldstones.

44. Possum Hollow, near St. James Church, owned by Mr. & Mrs. Leonard Myers (Mier) - 6 or more unmarked graves. These are all bricked up. Some of the brick vaults are shaped like mummy cases.

45. Watts Farm Cemetery, near St. James Church, along St. James-Smithville Road, owned by Mr. & Mrs. Merritt Fogwell. (Mrs. Fogwell was formerly Miss Mildred Watts.) Approximately 8 to 10 fieldstones.

46. Browne Cemetery, Quaker Neck, on Lankford Bay, home of Mr. & Mrs. John B. De Coursey.
Sacred to the memory of Edward Browne who lived respected and beloved, and died home. August 1813 (15) In the sixth year of his age. Footstone: E. B.
   Each lovely place shall him rest ore.
   For him the tear, be duly shed.

Beloved, till life can charm no more
An Mourn'd till pity's self be dead.
To the memory of Louisa Browne, born March 24th, 1810 Died in Christian hope
and assurance of a resurrection unto Eternal Life Sept. 22nd, 1852 7a yrs. 5
mo. and 29 days. The brothers and sisters of a beloved sister have erected
this monument of their affection.
Where shall the morn her earliest tears bestow.
Where first roses of the year shall blow;
While angels with their silver wings o're shade
The ground, now sacred by thy relics made.
                    H. Winternight maker of Balti.
Julia A. Browne consort of Edward Browne departed this life 18th of
September 1823 (aged) 42(?) years. Footstone: T. A. B.
May spring from thy spot of thy rest.
But no cypress or year let us see.
For why should we morn for the blest.
In memory of Edward Browne Born Jan'y. 7th 1804, Died Mar. 21st. 1857, Aged
53 years, 2 mos. and 14 days. Footstone: E. B.

47. Elmwood - The Davis Farm, near Still Pond, owned now by Mr. Prickett of
New Jersey.
Thomas C. Kennard, M. D. born Sep'r 14th, 1802 died Feb'y. 25, 1879.
Footstone: T. C. K. May he rest in Peace   H. Sisson & son Balti. Md.
Jane E. Hanson wife of Dr. Thomas C. Kennard Born July 1st, 1809 died Ash
Wednesday Feb'y. 7th, 1883. Requiescat in Pace. Footstone: J. E. K.
H. Sisson & son Balti., Md.
Thomas Kennard M. D. of St. Louis, Missouri Eldest son of Dr. Thomas C. &
Jane E. Kennard born June 1, 1834, Died Nov. 9, 1879
In memory of Laura Eldest child of Thomas & Jane Kennard Born July 28th,
1828 Died July 31st, 1854. Footstone: L. K.   H. Winternight maker,
Balt'o.
Charlie son of Thomas & Jane Kennard Born Dec. 22, 1820, Died Jan. 26, 1828
Cora H. daughter of Thomas & Jane Kennard born Apr. 30, 1838, Died Jun 8,
1844.
Frederick E. Son of Thomas & Jane Kennard Born May 25, 1841, Died July 29,
1841
Helen G. daughter of Thomas & Jane Kennard Born May 25, 1841, Died Oct. 1,
1845. Footstone: H. G. K.
James A. Kennard born Oct. 26th 1839. Fell at the moment of victory in the
battle of Bull Run July 19th, 1861. Talented, generous, and brave; May the
young Martyr's sacrifice be accepted. Footstone: J. A. K.
Francis Clement youngest son of Jane Elizabeth & Dr. Thomas C. Kennard born
June 3rd., 1856, Died Aug. 26, 1889. Footstone: F. C. K.
John Hanson Died July 4, 1826, Aged 14 years. Footstone

48. All stones at the Hayes Farm, which was also a Kennard Burial Ground,
have gone. Farm now owned by Mr. & Mrs. John Carville Sutton, near
Kennedyville, Md.

49. Moffett Cemetery on Galena-Chesterville Road, now owned by Mrs. Julia
Nicholson Jervis.
In memory of Elizabeth wife of George Morfet, (Moffett). She died January
1, 1775, Aged 36. Death has conquered me but I shall rise again And he
shall set me free. Footstone: E. M.

Also 3 fieldstones found.
A slave cemetery was found on the Moffett Farm - large spot, no stones, only sunken places in the ground.

50. Comegys Farm, near Crumpton, now owned by Mr. & Mrs. John Peacock, Black's Station-Chesterville Road. Cemetery lot in middle of field, trees and growth all around. One fieldstone.
In Memory of Benjamin Comegys, he died at sea on the 15th day of June 1809 in the 47th year of his age. At his urgent request, his remains were conveyed to this place by his friend, James Coche, M. D. and interred near those of his wife on the 21st of the same month.
In memory of Hannah daughter of Nathaniel and Hannah Comegys Born on the 26th day of January An Dom 1775, Married on the 6th day of January 1791 to Benjamin Comegys and departed this life on the 28th day of December in the same year, Age twenty one years eleven months and two days.
Ann daughter of John M. and Anna W. Comegys died March 6th, 1831 age 13 years. Footstone: A. C.
Maria C. daughter of John M. and Anna W. Comegys died April 20th, 1843 aged 3 years 2 mo's and 9 days.

51. Angelica Nursery near Chesterville, Md. now owned by Mr. Vernon Cole.
My husband - Thomas I. Mann died Sept. 15, 1852 In the 53d year of his age.
1 fieldstone.

52. Old Episcopal Cemetery near old Rectory outside of Massey, Md.
Edward R. Ryland Died Apr. 8, 1840 age 40 yrs. 3 mos. 25 d's.
In memory of Samuel Clothier who departed this life January 9th, 1832 aged 61 years (born 1772)
In memory of Elizabeth Murphy who departed this life May 10, 1806 age 36 years one month (born 1770)
One large fieldstone.

53. Ringgold's Fortune, or Violet Grove, Lankford Road & Ricaud's Branch Road.
In memory of Joseph M. Brown who died March 1845 aged 4 years.
Couple of fieldstones.
Ringgold's Fortune, was owned by the late Mr. Richard Hynson Rogers, now owned by Mr. Stefen Skipp.

54. Napley Green, Eastern Neck Island Road, formerly owned by Mr. DuPont, now owned by his four daughters. Two graves, bulldozed out, now building constructed on site where graves used to be. Note: no markers were found.

55. Ellendale, Eastern Neck Island Road.
Ringgolds and Willson's graveyard was east of the house. Several stones found opposite of house. Slabs, one woman and 2 children. The old house had to be abandoned because the Bay had just about washed it away.

56. Hynson Chapel on Baker's Lane and Ricaud's Branch Road and Lankford Road.
Sacred to the memory of George Coleman died Jan. 15th, 1867 aged 28 years (born 1839).

Ida P. daughter of Henry & Suzanna Bramble departed this life on August 12, 1863. These two graves are within a fence and the stones are in several pieces.

Sacred to the memory of John Bramble died March 27, 1869, aged 58 (born 1811)

Enoch Leatham died January 21, 1871 in the 51st year of his age. Gone but not forgotten.

Ellen Bure daughter of R. T. & Sarah A. Crew Died July 19, 1867, aged 4 yrs., 6 mos. 3 das.
  No more I clasp thee in my arms Nor nurse thy little head
  No more I watch thy gentle sleep For thy my child art dead.

Elizabeth F. daughter of Richard & Mary Jones died April 12th 1872, aged 18 years 3 mo's. eleven days.

Sarah R. daughter of Richard & Mary Jones died Febr. 3, 1879 Aged 37 years.
  Long and many were the pains she bore
  Slowly dissolved, the silver cord gave way
  And now tis broke, and mallines conflict ore.
  Heaven throws its portals wide, to endless days.

57. Cedar Hill formerly owned by George Lamb Bowers, near Smithville. The cemetery has disappeared; it was in the side yard.

58. Anthony Cemetery, on Mr. Clinton Riley's Farm near Galena, Md.
John Anthony, Q.M., 6 Pa. Mil., Rev War
5 other graves with field stones.
The mill property was transferred from Wayne Anthony and wife to Charles Gooding and wife, October 1857.

59. Cemetery on Mrs. Emory Camp's farm, near Galena, Md. 5 field stones.

60. Rich Level Farm, near Golts, owned by Mr. & Mrs. Olin Davis. About 25 fieldstones within a stone wall cemetery. This farm belonged in the Williams' family.

61. Blackiston Cemetery, North of Massey. All of the Blackiston family was removed to Shrewsbury Churchyard except this one:
In memory of Elizabeth Brown who departed this life on the 16th day of January 1823 in the 45 year of her age (born 1778). She was a servant for the family.

62. Slave Cemetery also on the Moffett or Jarrell Farm, Chesterville-Galena Road. A large area; nothing found except sunken places.

63. Wallis & Comegys Cemetery on Perkins Hill Road.
J. Wallis Boyer Died Sept. 1846, aged 14 months.
In memory of Francis L. Wallis died Apr. 7th, 1855 in the 51st year of his age. An honest man. The noble work of God. Footstone: F. L. W.
In memory of Emily Thomas wife of Francis L. Wallis Died March 2, 1896 in the 93rd year of her age.
  Grant her eternal rest Oh Lord
  And let light perpetual shine upon her.
A soldier of the Revolution Jesse Comegys son of William and Anne Comegys Born Oct. 1749 and Died Jan. 1804.

His wife Mary Everett Comegys daughter of Benjamin and Ann Everett Died Mar. 31, 1815, Aged 34 years 5 months (born Oct. 1780)

Infant daughter of Francis L. and Emily Wallis Feb'y 25, 1827. Footstone.

William John son of Francis L. and Emily Wallis Died May 25th, 1831 Aged 14 mos. and 5 days. Footstone: W. J. W.

Mary Emily daughter of Francis L. and Emily Wallis Died March 7th, 1841, Aged 18 mos. and 2 da's.

64.   Ashley Cemetery in Piney Neck, near Rock Hall.

Mary Ann beloved wife of David Ashley Born Oct. 18th, 1823, Died Jan. 9th, 1907.

    The precious one from us has gone
    Her voice we loved is still
    Her vacant chair is in our home
    Which never can be filled
    May her soul rest in heaven

David C. Ashley Born March 21, 1819, Died Dec. 7, 1911.

    Sleep on dear Father And after your rest with God.

Charles H. 1859-1945

Agnes 1861-1942

Rollison - Mary E. 1885-1957/John E. 1881-1947

Gilbert L. Ashley Md. Cox U. S. Coast Guard World War I, June 2, 1893 - Nov. 13, 1958.

David M. Hodges Jan. 23, 1895, June 12 1896

Our baby boy William Lewis Beck

In memory of Jeremiah Blanch who departed this life November 8th, 1824 In the 50th year of his age.

In memory of Anne daughter of Thomas T. and Jane Crouch Born June 12, 1874, Died Nov. 17, 1884.

    Father grieve not, Mother weep not
    Try to smooth your troubles o'er
    Think of her as only sleeping
    Not as dead, but gone before.

Emory P. Lister 1915-1925

William P. Lister 1889-1927

William Worton Born Aug. 22, 1803 departed this life Oct. 30th, 1850

Thomas Crouch 1836-1907

Jane Crouch 1840-1907

Elbourn - J. Thomas 1861-1948/Rebecca 1862-1946

John P. Middleton, Sr. 1853-1934

Mary Ellen beloved wife of John P. Middleton Born Feb. 24, 1862 Died Dec. 17, 1911. She sleeps, we leave her in peace to rest.

In memory of Ida daughter of James and Mary Dolan Born Oct. 30th, 1876, Died Apr. 1, 1879

John P. Dolan August 4th, 1819, August 30th, 1827. Gone but not forgotten, May his soul rest in peace.

In memory of Ellen Clyde daughter of George and Eleanor Sewell Born Nov. 8, 1874, Died Nov. 20, 1879.

Richard Crouch departed this life April 11, 1823.

Two larger fieldstones.

James F. Shriver Co. B. 2 E. F. Md. Inf.

Mary E. wife of James Dolan Born July 17, 1857, died Apr. 8, 1916.

    Rest on dear Mother thy labor o'er
    Thy willing hands will toil no more

A faithful Mother both true and kind
A truer mother you could not find.   Footstone: M. E. D.
Pretty thing 1950-63 Our Baby Doll. Note: this is a dog.
Phoebe G. Middleton wife of John P. Middleton daughter of David C. and Mary
Ashley Born Dec. 9, 1856 died Mary 14, 1883, Aged 28 years 5 mo's. 5 da's.
    Farewell, farewell our sister dear
    Life is sad, without you here
    O may we meet in heaven above
    Where all is peace and joy and love.
    Gone but not forgotten.

65. Mrs. Scott Beck's Farm called the Dunn Farm in Broad Neck. Tenant –
Mr. Ernest Potts. Found traces of brick in driveway by the side of the
barn. Under nearby tree a large slab removed from a vault. Inscription and
epitaph: Martha Ann the wife of James Dunn who departed this life on
February 6th in the year of our Lord 1752 – age 18 years 2 months and 8
days.
    Death thou has conquered me
        In the days and hours
    But Christ shall conquer thee
        And I shall live again.
    Time falters not the hour
        The just shall walk and sing
    Oh, grave where is thy power
        Oh, death where is thy sting?

66. Farm belonging to David Bramble called Gresham near Tolchester. A
private burying ground one time was located on knoll in middle of field by
the bay. Mrs. Bramble says people remember stones being there with the
names of Gresham and Ayres families, who were the early settlers. The
Brambles have not been able to find a stone anywhere.

67. Farm next to Hopewell Corner near Worton (Tilden Cooper Farm). Mrs.
Bertha Miller Cooper (Lane) present owner said the private burying ground
was right back of the house, where a telephone pole now stands. One piece
of tombstone lying under an old windmill had this: WM. Perkins aged 63
years. Blessed are the dead which die in the Lord.

68. Back of the Old Kennedyville School House. We found 5 old fieldstones.
Several looked like they had somthing marked on them. A little grove of
trees stands over the triangle shaped plot. Some say the Ireland family is
buried here, Mr. Charlie Ireland being the last to live in the area. Mr.
Hope Hudson (1971) remembers fieldstones and markers on the plot. He
remembers several stones with the name Hudson and one with the name Price.
It has been called the Scone farm, his grandfather John Munro Hudson lived
there. It now belongs to a Mr. McHenry.

69. We visited Marsh Point behind Locust Grove, owned by the Deringer and
Bryan families. The land belonging to Isaac Freeman at one time, a famous
Maryland politician, and Mrs. Bryan's great-great-great-great-great
grandfather. A pile of field stones are piled against a tree in the back of
the old Isaac Freeman house at Marsh Point. The house was built by William
Pearce who bought the land in 1678 from Godfrey Harman. Isaac Freeman
bought it in 1736 from Andrew Pearce.

70. Benjamin McGuire farm near Still Poind, next to Lamb's Meadow. The farmhouse in back burned in 1928. Mr. Raymond Carrington says there was a slave burying ground south of the house. The farm is called Swarthmore.

71. Baxter Farm (1971) west of Smithville, land originally owned by the Parsons family (John, Lewis, Isaac and Harrison Parsons). A family burying ground for the Parsons, one time in the middle of the field on corner, about 500 feet from the road. No remains. Mr. Robert Usilton remembers it.

72. Old Salem church burying ground on Millard Joiner farm (1971) near Melitota across from Columbia Manor and near old Melitota School. No remains. Mr. Roland Corey remembers when there were a dozen fieldstones, around 1920.

73. Sunrise Farm near Chesterville, owned by Mrs. Stanley Townsend of Odessa, Delaware.
Jester Family –
In memory of Jonathan Jester Jun son of Jonathan Jester Born 11th of May 1781 and died 4th of August 1800 – A faithful and promising youth 19 years 2 months 25 days. Jonathan was supposed to be injured by his application to fortitude.
    In early life before the bud was blown,
    Best of success to make a part his own.
In memory of William U., Jester Born 11th day of May 1774 and died the 2nd of October 1800 26 years 4 months and 21 days son of Jonathan Jester
In Memory of Jonathan Jester who departed this life the 28th of September 1805 – aged 57 years 27 days. He lived in the practice of all local duties of son, husband, father, friend. In his pursuits of loyalty and enterprise the dealings honorable and punctual. He gave employment to the industrious and bread to the indigent. A useful member of society. And died, resigned and fully trusting In mercies of redeeming love. Note: (born Sept. 1, 1748)

74. Old Methodist Cemetery at Massey, Mr. and Mrs. Hynson E. Cole:
Eliza R. wife of Joseph N. Money Died March 30, 1865, Aged 43 years 11 days, Born Mar. 19, 1822.
Joseph N. Money departed this life Sept. 23, 1828, In the 38 year of his age.
Charles H. Humphry died April 25, 1881, Aged 37 years.
Tempy Ann Liza wife of Benjamin Hazel Died October 3rd. 1866 aged 38 years 9 months 13 days. She is not dead but sleeps.
Mary F. Daughter of John F. and Hennella Voshell died June 21 , 1888 aged 1 month
Infant son of William C. and Margaret Meginnis Died May 22, 1853.
To the memory of my beloved father Wm. C. Meginnis May 28, 1821, May 25, 1881. Gone but not forgotten. Stone marker, Hanson, Chestertown
Jesse S. son of W. C. Kennard and of Margaret Meginnis Died July 11, 1862 – aged 2 mons. 8 days.
Annie O. daughter of William C. and Margaret Magginnis Died July 8, 1860 aged 5 mos. and 7 days.
Edwinn son of William Maginnis Died Feb. 18, 1850, Aged 1 year 8 months 27 days.
Willie G. son of William and Margaret Maginnis Died Feb. 22, 1847 Aged 5 months 1 day.

Mary J. wife of Edward W. Spears Died June 26, 1870, Aged 22 years 1 mos. 1 day. I am the Resurrection and the Life.
Agnes daughter of William and Mary Maginnis Died May 23, 1812, Age 1 yr. 4 mos. 23 days
Margaret J. wife of Charles R. Hackett died april 10, 1871, Aged 77 years 3 mos. and 19 days.
Charles Hackett died March 16, 1862, aged 58 years 9 months and 7 days. Though lost sight to memory dear Mary.
Anna Mary daughter of Henry & Sibbella Hackett died July 5, 1841, aged 5 months.
To the memory of Sarah Ann daughter of Thomas and Margaret J. Numbers and wife of Samuel Coverdale departed this life Dec. 3, 1858, aged 40 years.
Henrietta – daughter of Geo. & Frances Hazel died May 27th, 1859 aged 20 years 6 mos.
James M. Cummerford 1833–1911. At Rest.
R. Money   10th 1865. Only part of the stone remains.
William T. Voshell died November 1st, 1882, aged 33 years, 4 months and 7 days. Footstone: W. T. V.
Thomas H. Voshell died May 18th, 1881 in the 65th year of his age.
    Here lies a kind husband father dear
        His God's will he should be here
    We hope our loss will be his gain
        In hoping heaven he may obtain.
At Rest. Footstone: T. H. V.
Sarah A. Voshell Died May 1, 1896 in her 75th year.
    You have left us dearest mother
        And can never return again
    You have left us with all our sorrows
        And our hearts are filled with pain.   Footstone: S. A. V.
75.   Old Hynson Chapel, Ricaud's branch and Route 20.
Maria Harris wife of William Harris daughter of Doct. James A. Anderson died July 3, 1817, aged 42 years and 7 months. Footstone: M. H. born 1-1775
Anna M. wife of Samuel Mansfield died Jan. 31, 1841, aged about 50 years. Footstone: A. M. M. born 1790
Samuel Mansfield Died January 31, 1837, aged about 37 years. Footstone: S. M. born 1800
In memory of Mary Ida daughter of Edmond and Mary I. Mansfield Born Sept. 27th, 1852, Died Mar. 8th, 1854. Suffer little children to come unto Me.
About 35 fieldstones.

76.   Overton Farm, Eastern Neck Island Road – Mr. & Mrs. Robert Strong.
In memory of Jane Copper Born Dec. 17th 1767, Died Feb. 25th, 1852, aged Eighty four years 2 months and 7 days. In hopes of blessed immortality. Footstone: J. C.
In Memory of Mary Hellen wife of Shadrach Watkins died Aug. 18th 1854, aged 15 years 7 mos. 3 weeks 5 days.
    Dearest wife thou hast left me
        We on earth no more shall meet
    But in heaven I hope to meet thee
        When life has past.   marker "Meridith"

77.   Aiello Farm, on Eastern Neck, between the road and Church Creek.
The Willson Family:
A field of daffodils mark the place where graves were once located.

78. Back of the Methodist Church in Rock Hall, Md. used in the 1800's.
William Scone who departed this life March 3rd, 1846 aged 53. (born 1793)
Marker: "Earle"
Many stones removed or covered over.
One large fieldstone.

79. Butchers Neck on Route 291, farm owned by Mrs. Jessie Jarrell. Mrs.
Jarrel says her sister remembers when the last one was buried at Butchers
Neck, 92 years ago. A Mrs. McClarey (McCleary) was buried there, where
daffodils now grow on her grave. At one time there was a fieldstone on her
grave, but no longer.

80. Grays Inn Point Farm near Rock Hall, resident of Edgar Strong. The
Graham family burying ground is back of the house. No trace of the graves.

81. Hodges Crouch, Skinners Neck near Rock Hall. The farm belonged to the
Grant family originally. At one time there were 8 or 10 graves in center of
the field, now gone. One stone is remembered: Mary A. Grant Consort of
Richard E. Grant died 1825. Last to be buried there was Jim Elburn.

82. Piney Neck Bible School. Stones have been removed. One person
remembers the name Crieghton on a child's stone.

83. Drum Point Farm near Rock Hall, owned at one time by Lloyd family,
Glenn's, MacCubbins, now Colonel Lloyd Cross. At one time there was a grave
yard by the side of the house, some fieldstones in front of the old barn
(moved there?). Two names remembered: John B. Glenn and George Glenn.

84. Near Haddaway's store (1971), Lynch. At Lynch near corner across from
R. W. Stavely's on the right stood an old house, occupied at one time by the
Lynch family. At the side of the house were large stones with the name
Chapman on them. It was bulldozed out and stones dumped into basement of an
old house and covered over.

Our mother In memory of Mary Amanda wife of James W. Chapman and only child
of William and Mary Webb born Oct. 19, 1837, died April 28, 1886. There is
rest in Heaven.

85. Farm belonging to T. R. Jones, Page Farm Plot, Tolchester-Rock Hall
Road.
Here lies the body of Mrs. Elizabeth Page who departed this life on the 14th
day of August 1773 Aged 59 years.
Here lies the body of Ralph Page who departed this life on the 4th day of
August 1773 Aged 63 years.
Sacred to the Memory - Here lies the body of Doctr Henry Page Vinled vin
Lorith Calearda Sinel (t?) of (S?) nnibu (nnivu?) Who departed this life
April 26, 1821 in the 50th year of his life.

86. Sprys Landing Farm, Route 291, owned (1971) by Ralph Bateman.
Approximately 1 mile west of Route 290 on Millington Road, turn towards the
river into Bateman's driveway. The house is 1/2 miles or so from the road.
Juliana daughter of John and Mary Woodland and wife of Gideon Pearce born
Mar. 14, 1788, died Feb. 8, 1809. Also: Edward son of G. and J. Pearce born

Nov. 20, 1808, died Aug. 1, 1809. This stone was in a little wood by the Chester River.

87. Quaker burying ground at Lynch.
Site of Cecil Friend's Meeting House where our forebears found divine guidance and executed a lasting influence to the community. 1696-1900.
Mary Ann Swann daughter of Wm. F. and Georgianna Swann born April 16, 1876, died June 1, 1896.
Martha E. Turner born 12th mo. 28th day 1840, died 11th mo. 16th day 1911

Quakerism on the Eastern Shore by Kenneth Carroll
Howard H. Parrott son of George Richard & Elma Bowers Hopkins Parrott born Dec 31, 1877, died Aug. 21, 1903.
Mary Rebecca Bowers, Parrott Usilton dau. of William and Sarah Lamb Bowers born Aug. 5, 1812, died Sept. 9, 1887.
Charles W. Warren born Nov. 4, 1835, died Oct. 24, 1885.
Mamie B. Warren dau. of Charles W. and Sarah Lamb Parrott Warren born 24th 12th mo. 1865, died 21st 2nd mo. 1870.
Sarah Lamb Parrott, dau. of Benjamin & Mary Rebecca Bowers Parrott, and wife of Charles W. Warren born Oct. 27, 1833, died Sept. 1, 1887.
Lillie Bowers Parrott, dau. of George Richard and Elma Bowers Hopkins Parrott born Dec. 8, 1875, died Dec. 31, 1938.
Emily May Parrott, dau. of George Richard and Elma Bowers Hopkins Parrott born Oct. 8, 1872, died Mar. 22, 1929.
George Elwood Parrott, son of George Richard Parrott and Elma Bowers Hopkins Parrott born Feb. 24, 1869, died July 19, 1926.
Elma Bowers Hopkins wife of George Richard Parrott Born Nov. 25, 1843, Died Apr. 29, 1930.
George Richard Parrott, son of Benjamin & Mary Rebecca Bowers Parrott born March 1, 1838, died August 26, 1898.
Harrie Wilson Parrott, son of George Richard & Elma Bowers Hopkins Parrott Born July 31, 1882, died Aug. 19, 1882.
Willie Benjamin Parrott, son of George Richard & Elma Bowers Hopkins Parrott. Born Nov. 4, 1870, died Nov. 23, 1870.
John Ellwood Parrott, son of George Richard & Elma Bowers Hopkins Parrott Born Aug. 7, 1867, Died Nov. 7, 1868.
Benjamin William Bowers Parrott, son of Benjamin and Mary Rebecca Bowers Parrott Born 9/11/1838, Died 10 mo. 13th 1856.

Cecil Meeting in S. E. Corner. 5 fieldstones. One footstone: A. B. M. One headstone: D. L. aged 74 years.
Rosamond Bowers 1841 age 63 years.
Joseph Turner died 8th day 6 mo. 1841 age 76 years.
Sara Turner died 6 mo. 8th da 1845.
Mary J. B. Daughter of Noll and Samuel M. Pennell died age 13 years 2 mos.
Sallie J. daughter of Noll and Samuel Pennell died Nov 16, 1869 aged 9 years 16 days.
Robert Pennell son of Noll and Samuel Born Sept. 6, 1854, Died Nov. 15, 1872.
Rebecca Turner born 1845 died 1908.
Elizabeth Turner born 1826, died 1903.
Richard T. Turner born 1819, died 1892.
Richard B. Turner born 1811, died 1900.
Elizabeth Thomas born June 15, 1810, died Mar. 30, 1875.

Harry son of Noll and Samuel Pennell died Aug. 8, 1868, age 1 mo. 11 da's.
Margaret E. Usilton born 1801, died 1858.
James B. Holding born Oct. 12, 1805, died Apr. 15, 1884.
About 20 fieldstones.
Mary E. wife of John E. Baldwin died Apr. 16, 1851 in the 40th year of her age.
R. Lamb age 76
Robert Lamb born 1828 died 1851.
Fieldstone: R. D.   J. D.
Mary Ann Lamb Alston Norris born 1801 died Aug. 8, 1866, dau. of Joab and Hannah Lamb Alston and wife of John Cowman Norris.
Susan Allston Norris, dau. of John Cowman and Mary Ann Lamb Alston Norris born Nov. 28, 1827, died Feb. 15, 1850.
Daniel Lamb Norris, son of John Cowman and Mary Ann Lamb Alston Norris Born Sept. 30, 1834, Died July 7, 1851.
William Bowers, son of Thomas and Ann Bowers Born Jan. 12, 1778, Died
Sarah Lamb Bowers, dau. of John & Mary Lamb, and wife of William Bowers Born July 19, 1784, Died Aug. 4, 1823.
Rebecca Lamb, dau. of John & Mary Lamb Born 1773, Died Dec. 23, 1846. Kent News.
Ann Elizabeth Bowers Allen, dau. of William and Sarah Lamb Bowers Born Apr. 16, 1805, Died Oct. 21, 1870. Wife of Dr. R. T. Allen. Kent News.
William Lamb Bowers, son of William and Sarah Lamb Bowers. Born Aug. 5, 1816, Died May 13, 1887.
John Lamb Bowers, son of William and Sarah Lamb Bowers Born Mar. 19, 1807, Died Nov. 1, 1878.
Anne E. Bowers, Bowers, dau. of John and Rosamond Lamb Bowers, & wife of John Lamb Bowers Born Aug. 31, 1808, Died Jun 18, 1881.
Ann R. Bowers Melvin, dau. of James Lamb and Rebecca Reed Bull Bowers, and wife of Thomas W. Melvin Born Aug. 8, 1848, Died Jan. 16, 1882.
Rosamond Melvin, dau. of Thomas W. & Ann R. Bowers Melvin Born Dec. 23, 1867, Died Sept. 8, 1871.
Thomas Lamb, son of Thomas Alexander and Susan Lamb Maslin Lamb. Born Sept. 22, 1853, Died 1879.
Walter R. Neall, son of Sarah R. Bowers Neall Born Aug. 3, 1848, Died Sept. 28, 1879.
John B. Neall, son of Sarah R. Bowers Neall Born Dec. 17, 1844, Died Apr. 28, 1852.
David B. Neall, son of Sarah R. Bowers Neall, Born 1835, Died 1851.
Robert Thomas Parrott, son of Benjamin & Mary Rebecca Bowers Parrott Born July 31, 1844, Died Aug. 31, 1851. Quakerism on the Eastern Shore.
Benjamin Parrott, son of Aaron & Rachel Parrott of Talbot Co. Maryland Born Aug. 16, 1799, Died Nov. 21, 1846. Kent News.
Hannah Lamb Atkinson, dau. of Pearce & Rachel George Lamb, and wife of William Atkinson Born Sept. 2, 1773, Died Jan. 20, 1851. Headstone: L. L. aged 74.
Daniel Lamb, son of George & Rebecca Corse Lamb and Husband of Mary Lamb Dawson Born Mar. 23, 1779, Died Apr. 22, 1853.
Mary Ann Bowers Needles, dau. of John and Rosamond Lamb Bowers, and wife of John Needles, son of Edward & Mary Lamb Needles Born 1799, Died Apr. 7, 1879.
James Lamb Bowers, son of John and Rosamond Lamb Bowers Born 2nd mo. 7th 1810, Died 1st mo. 4th 1882.

Rebecca Reed Bull Bowers, dau. of Isaac & Ann Webster Bull Born 3rd mo. 12th, 1826, Died 4th mo. 17th, 1916.
William L. Bowers, son of James Lamb and Rebecca Reed Bull Bowers, Born Feb. 18, 1868, Died Aug. 29, 1916.
John Bowers, son of Thomas & Ann Bowers Born Nov. 20, 1767, Died Nov. 13, 1820.
John Bowers, Jr. son of John & Rosamond Lamb Bowers, Born 1804, Died 1830.
David William Bowers, son of John & Rosamond Lamb Bowers Born 1813, Died 1834.
Elizabeth Bowers, dau. of John & Rosamond Lamb Bowers Born 1802, Died Mar. 14, 1841.

88. Haddaway Chapel, Broad Neck. This burying ground is where once stood a Methodist church. When it closed, it was moved to Rock Hall and made into a home. It is called Haddaways Chapel. It is on the right hand side of Lankford Bay Road between a colored settlement and the road going back to Billy Nicholson's farm.
In Memory William J. Fletcher 1859-1901.
Mother/Father Herbert Fletcher 1865-1925   Sadie Fletcher 1884-1925
Susan & S. J. daughter Fletcher
Wm. B. Bennett Born Nov. 1831, Died Oct. 19, 1880, Age 59 yrs. 5 das.
John W. Haddaway Mar. 8, 1835, Dec. 10, 1874.
Joseph B. son of Joseph B. and Mary E. Haddaway Died Nov. 1878 aged 4 yrs. 6 mos.
In Memory of Father & Mother - John E. Vickers 1849-1908 Sarah E., his wife, 1854-1893
Julia daughter of Sarah & W. O. Fletcher Died July 19, 1872, Age 5 years 10 months 8 days. At Rest in Heaven.
Lawrence D. Maslin Died May 30, 1862, Age 2 yrs. 4 mos.
Nettie M. Maslin Died June 9, 1862, Age 4 years 4 mo.
Richard Born son of Edward & Ann Haddaway born June 22, 1841, died March 21, 1865, aged 23 yrs. and 9 mos.
Edward Haddaway beloved son of Edw. & Ann Haddaway Born April 10, 1830, Died Oct. 10, 1854, Age 24 years 6 months.
Emma Kendall born May 7, 1866, died June 4, 1888, age 22 yrs.
In Memory of Ann E. beloved of A. Kendall
Luther H. infant son of Luther A. and Ann Kendall born Nov. 3, 1861, died Dec. 12, 1866. We have lost one child an angel.

89. Around Tommy Haddaway's store on the corner at Lynch were found some tombstones. Mr. Bob Usilton says they were moved there by Rosa when he owned the adjoining place. He says it was called the Copper Farm. He remembers a Med Copper living there.
Footstone: M. A. C.
Another stone: William Webb departed this life December 1861 in the 21 years 1 month of age.

90. Morris farm. No evidence of the cemetery; at one time it had name stones. The Morris and Shepperd families were buried there. On the Hurlock's Corner - Golts Road.
    Across the road is a destroyed cemetery. The name stones contained more of the Morris family. No further evidence.

91. Clayton Cemetery. Taken to the cemetery by William C. Clayton of Golts. The cemetery is located about 2 miles south of Golts on Black top road. The left hand side is near the Maryland - Delaware line. Fieldstones. In the first row is buried Jacob Clayton, who was born about 1789. He was the great grandfather of William Clayton (who is 81 years old). Also in the first row are two Budd graves (they married into the Clayton family). Also three children of Mr. & Mrs. Nicholas George. One of the children was born in 1864. Three died before they were 15.

92. Wilmer Farm, on Perkins Hill Road. The Wilmer family is buried here. Old Mr. Phil Wilmer's twin brother is buried here.

93. a. Thornton Farm, on Perkins Hill Road, owned by Mrs. Jane Brooks Sprinkle. We found a hole where a grave was. About 1/4 acres. About 20 to 25 fieldstones.

    b. Also on this farm is a slave cemetery. No signs.

94. Quinn Farm. North of Massey on Quinn Road. This is the Greenwood Cemetery. It contains 2 marker stones, fieldstones, unmarked graves. Hannah - wife of Joseph Greenwood died July 18, 1866. Footstone: H. G.

95. Remington Farms. Burying ground of the Hynsons and Dunns, now gone - a wildlife cage was built on the ground.

96. Irving Tillnian Miller Burying Ground.

97. Spring Cove - Miller Burying Ground and Downey Burying Ground, Rock Hall.

98. Graveyards washed into bay at Huntingfield and Spring Hill, Rock Hall.

99. On the Old Griffith Farm near Sassafras, granted in 17th century to Richard Lake. John George died about 1747. The farm was called Adventure. A small grave plot, one stone (there were others): Consecrated to the memory of Mrs. Elizabeth (Baird) Johns who departed this life December 18, 1816 aged Fifty-six years.

100. On the farm belonging to Mr. Munyon.
B. Meginnis born Feb. 26, 1771, died Jan. 23, 1815.
Geo. McGinnis died Dec. 29, 1829, age Forty-three years, 1 mo. and 18 days.

101. Baker Graveyard on Bakers Lane along road. Some of it was under the road, across from Theodore Redman and George Redman's farm. The farm belongs to Mrs. Catherine Gilpin Johnson.

102. Robert R. Hatcherson Farm. Graveyard along Bakers Lane, north of Route 20 (1/3 mile) - one grave with name of Strong. A small plot under a wild cherry tree name was Yoates. Mr. Hatcherson found some wooden markers when he moved there.

103. Dr. Howard Dana's Farm, Radcliffe Cross, Quaker Neck Road. When plowing a workman uncovered 7 vaults. Dr. Dana replaced all parts. He learned that a Smythe family was buried here.

104. Slave cemetery at the Blackiston Farm, near Massey. The farm now belongs to William Moffett.
Granger 1838   Wife - Mary Blackiston
Husband - David Blackiston.

105. Clayton Hick' Farm on N. 213. A graveyard abaout 500 feet from the highway. Mr. Hicks said he was told the name was Yoates. He found wooden markers there when he moved to Goose Hill Farm. Also Jarrell Family.

106. Back of Mrs. Julia Skirven. Rock Hall - there was a cemetery at one time. The Maslin family lived there.

107. Briscoe Cemetery. Massey on the Delaware line Road, close to the Episcopal Manse.
George A. Briscoe departed this life on May 23, 1847 aged 50 years.
Margaret D. wife of George A. Briscoe May 26, 1847, aged 36 years.
Note: George A. Briscoe was a son of Daniel Briscoe.

108. Wickes. Burying ground on the Harold Hill farm near Edesville. Two large marble stones.

109. Edes Cemetery, at Simns Jacquette farm, Edesville. There are several graves and fieldstones.

110. Hodges-Crouch burying ground. Burying ground for the Grant family, Skinners Neck.

Indexed is the number of the paragraph NOT the page number. Dates of birth
(b), death (d), place of burial and other information derived from the text
and OTHER sources.

l
ı o

l

Jov

ɔh

d
of

l8;

ı o

87

a

,

,

7,
ri

n

Indexed is the number of the paragraph NOT the page number. Dates of birth (b), death (d), place of burial and other information derived from the text and OTHER sources.

BAIRD Elizabeth 99
BAKER Anna Eliza 23 (b 12-12-1799; d
5-5-1862; dau of Thomas & Margaret
Baker; m Edwin World Maslin)
BAKER Graveyard 101 (Family burial
ground along Baker's Lane, opposite
Redman farm. 1971 owner: Mrs.
Catherine Gilpin Johnson)
BAKER Margaret 23
BAKER Thomas 23
BALDWIN John E. 87 (wife: Mary E.)
BALDWIN Mary E. 87 (b 1811; d
4-16-1851 in her 40th yr)
BARROLL John (In 1971 family lived on
part of "Knock's Folly." Small old
burial gorund there; see paragraph 34)
BARROLL family 22
BARROLL L. Wethered 9 (co-author of
"Wethered Book" with Brandon Barringer
- 1967)
BARROLL Morris K. 16
BATCHELOR HOPE FARM 36 (Regester
family burial ground; home of Robert
M. Hewes family)
BATEMAN Ralph 86
BAXTER Farm 71
BECK James of George 42 (b 1798; d
10-29-1882, aged 84; wife - Mary Jane)
BECK Mary 42 (b 1798; d 10 -29-1882,
aged 84)
BECK Mary Jane 42
BECK Mrs. Scott 65 (1971 owner of the
Dunn farm)
BECK William Lewis 64 ("Our Baby Boy"
- no dates)
BENNETT William B. 88 (b 1831; d
10-19-1880, age 59 years, 5 days)
BLACKISTON Cemetery 61 (Family moved
to Shrewsbury Churchyard, leaving one
grave, that of a servant)
BLACKISTON David 104 (wife: Mary)
BLACKISTON Farm 104
BLACKISTON Mary 104 (wife of David)
BLANCH Jeremiah 64 (b 1774; d
11-8-1824, in his 50th yr)
BLAY Catherine 9 (dau of Wm. &
Isabella)
BLAY Charles Tilden 16
BLAY Colonel Edward 9 (donor of burial
ground at Blay's Range in 1709, on
route 213 near Shrewsbury Church)

BLAY Dr. William 16
BLAY Edward 9 (son of Wm. & Isabella)
BLAY Issabella 9 (dau of Wm. &
Isabella)
BLAY Issabella Pearce 9 (dau of Col.
Pearce & wife of Wm. Blay)
BLAY Mary B. 16
BLAY Rachel 9 (dau of Wm. & Isabella;
m(1) Peregrine Brown; m(2) Edward
Scott; m(3) Aquila Paca
BLAY William 9 (son of Wm. & Isabella)
BLAY William 9 (only son of Col.
Edward & wife Ann; m Isabella Pearce)
BLOECHER Georgia 23
BORDLEY Catherine 22 (b 1776; d
1-26-1838, age 62, bur Worton Manor)
BORDLEY John 22 (b 1764; d 12-21-1815,
age 51, bur Worton Manor)
BOTHE Berthold 25
BOUVIER Jacqueline Lee 23
BOUVIER Janet Lee 23
BOUVIER John Vernon 23
BOUVIER John Vernon II 23
BOUVIER John Vernon III 23
BOUVIER Maude Frances Sargeant 23
BOWERS Ann 87
BOWERS Ann R. 87 (b 8-8-1848; d
1-16-1882; dau of James L. & Rebecca
Reed Bull Bowers; m 5-12-1867 Thomas
W. Melvin)
BOWERS Ann Elizabeth 87 (b 4-16-1805;
d 10-21-1870; dau of Wm. & Sarah Lamb
Bowers; m 2-5-1828 Dr. Robert T. Allen
of Harford Co)
BOWERS Anne E. 87 (b 831-1808; d
6-18-1883; dau John & Rosamond Lamb
Bowers; m John Lamb Bowers)
BOWERS David William 87 (b 4-17-1813;
d 4-22-1834; son of John & Rosamond
Lamb Bowers)
BOWERS Elizabeth 87 (b 3-7-1802; d
3-14-1841; dau of John & Rosamond Lamb
Bowers)
BOWERS George Lamb 57 (b 10-20-1856;
4-26-1943; single; once owned "Cedar
Hill." Cemetery in side yard has
disappeared.)
BOWERS James Lamb 87 (b 2-7-181-; d
1-10-1882; m in 1830's Rebecca Lowes,
who d 10-3-1842; m(2) 9-21-1845

Rebecca Reed Bull, b 9-26-1826, d 4-17-1912)

BOWERS John 87 (b 11-20-1766; d 11-13-1820; son of Thomas & Ann Bowers)

BOWERS John Jr. 87 (b 3-7-1804; d 10---1830; son of John & Rosamond Lamb Bowers)

BOWERS John Lamb 87 (b 3-19-1807; d 11-1-1878; son of Wm. & Sarah Lamb Bowers; m Ann E. Bowers)

BOWERS Major James 21

BOWERS Mary Ann 87 (b 7-13-1799; d 4-7-1879; dau of John & Rosamond Lamb Bowers; 3rd wife of John Needles m 9-1-185-)

BOWERS Mary Rebecca 87 (b 8-5-1816; d 9-9-1887; m(1) Benjamin Parrott; m(2) Joseph Usilton)

BOWERS Rebecca Reed Bull 87 (b 1826; d 1912; m James Lamb Bowers)

BOWERS Rosamond Lamb 87 (b 7-25-1778; d 11-27-1841; dau of John & Mary Lamb; m 5-12-1796 John Bowers, son of Thomas & Ann Pearce Bowers, brother of William)

BOWERS Rosamond 87

BOWERS Sarah 21 (b 11-11-1768; d 7-15-1818; age 49 yrs, 9 mo. 4 days; wife of Major James Bowers)

BOWERS Sarah Lamb 87 (b 7-19-1784; d 8-4-1823; m 1804 William Bowers, dau of John & Mary Lamb)

BOWERS Thomas 87

BOWERS William 87 (b 1-12-1778; d 9-20-1830; m 1804 Sarah Lamb; son of Thomas & Ann Pearce Bowers)

BOWERS William Lamb 87 (b 8-5-1816; d 5-13-1887; single; son of Wm. & Sarah Lamb Bowers; twin of Mary Rebecca Bowers Parrott)

BOWERS William L. 87 (b 2-18-1868; d 8-29-1916; m 1-4-1893 Mary A. Stevenson; lived in Del.)

BOYER Agnes 39 (b 1826; d 6-1-1902; age 76; wife of Stephen Boyer)

BOYER Agnes 39 (b 1866; d 8-4-1866; age 5 mo. 9 days, dau of Wm. & Kate Boyer)

BOYER Catherine J. 39 (b 1837; d 4-27-1871; age 34 years; wife of Wm. Boyer)

BOYER J. Wallis 63 (b July 1845; d 9-1846, age 14 mo.)

BOYER Kate 39

BOYER Maria 39 (b 1800; d 12-21-1854; age 54 years, 8 mo., 20 days)

BOYER Maria A. 39 (b 1-15-1825; d 6-3-1899)

BOYER Richard T. 39 (b 1817; d 4-20-1857, in his 40th yr; wife: Sophia)

BOYER Sophia 39 (b 1832; d 9-12-1860, in her 28th yr, wife of Richard T. Boyer)

BOYER Stephen 38 (b 1777; d 2-21-1838; aged 61 yrs, 4 mo., 18 days; wife - Maria b 1800)

BOYER Stephen 39 (b 3-31-1828; d 4-12-1904; wife: Agnes Boyer)

BOYER Stephen 38 (gave St. Clements Church Farm to the Parish - Massey)

BOYER Urie Irving 39 (b 1816; d 1-30-1855; aged 39 yrs , 2 mo. 19 days)

BOYER William 39 (b 1831; d 9-14-1885; age 54; wife: Catherine)

BRAMBLE David 66

BRAMBLE Henry 56 (wife: Suzanna; dau: Ida P. d 8-12-1863)

BRAMBLE Ida P. 56 (d 8-12-1863)

BRAMBLE John 56 (b 1811; d 3-27-1869; aged 58)

BRAMBLE Suzanna 56 (wife of Henry (above)

BRICE Emma S. 18 (b 9-5-1858; d 7-13-1921)

BRICE George H. 18 (d 2-21-1874, in his 31st yr)

BRICE James 18 (b 1-8-1780; d 5-28-1825, age 45 yrs, 4 mo., 20 days)

BRICE James Richard 18 (b 11-12-1821; d 9-12-1823, age 1 yr, 11 mo.)

BRICE Mary Ann 18 (wife of William A. Brice; mother of Nathaniel who d 1869)

BRICE Sally Ann Elizabeth 18 (b 1-31-1813; d 2-15-1814, age 1 yr, 15 days)

BRICE William A. 18 (father of Nathaniel d 1869)

BRICE William As 18
BRICE William Nathaniel 18 (b
12-9-1838; d 7-23-1869, age 31 yrs, 7
mo., 14 days; son of Wm. A. & Mary Ann
Brice
BRISCOE Cemetery 107
BRISCOE Daniel 107 (father of George
A. who d 1847)
BRISCOE George A. 107 (b 1797; d May
23, 1847, aged 50 years; wife of
Margaret D. Briscoe
BRISCOE Margaret D. 107(b 1811; d
5-26-1847; bur near Episcopal manse,
near Massey, with above Briscoes.)
BRISCOE Mr. and Mrs. William 31
("Buttonwood," near Galena, is Mrs.
Briscoe's birthplace. She grew up
there with her grandparents, Rev &
Mrs. Prettyman.)
BRITAIN Jane 23 (m Thomas Maslin in
London)
BRITISH soldiers 20
BROOKS Farm 93
BROWN C. C. 5 (b 7-13-1821; d
4-21-1865 (Cornelius C.))
BROWN Edward 14 (husband of Sarah S.
Brown)
BROWN Edward C. 5 (b 2-10-1810; d
9-28-1831)
BROWN Edward C. 5 (b 7-2-1855; d
9-15-1855; son of C. C. & Lizzie T.
Brown)
BROWN Elizabeth 61 (b 1778; d Jan.
1823, in her 45th year, servant of the
Blackiston family)
BROWN Elizabeth Thomas 5 (b 6-23-1856;
d 1-14-1903)
BROWN Hiram 5 (b 8-3-1814; d
5-18-1864)
BROWN Hiram 5 (b 1780; d 6-7-1848)
BROWN John 2 (Family Bible)
BROWN John 9 (1st husband of Rachel
Blay)
BROWN Joseph M. 53 (b 1841; d
3----1845, age 4, bur at Ringgold's
Fortune)
BROWN Lizzie T. 5 (b 6-30-1829; d
7-23-1903; wife of C. C. Brown)
BROWN Mary 5 (b 9-1-1786; d 10-5-1825;
consort of Hiram Brown)

BROWN May Ida 5 (b 12-5-1863; d
5-27-1891; wife of Thomas T. Brown)
BROWN Peregrine 9 (name given on stone
as 1st husband of Rachel Blay but
actual name of husband was John)
BROWN Peregrine 9 (son of Rachel Blay
Brown)
BROWN Rachel 9
BROWN Rachel Blay 9 (wife of Peregrine
or John Brown)
BROWN Sarah S. 14 (b 11-13-1803; d
4-4-1874; wife of Edward Brown)
BROWN Thomas F. 5 (b 1-21-1854; d
9-25-1855; son of C. C. & Lizzie T.
Brown)
BROWN Thomas T. 5 (wife: May Ida
Brown, b Elmira, N.Y.; d in Brooklyn)
BROWN William U. 5 (b 6-12-1789; d
9-12-1861)
BROWNE Cemetery 46 (on the John B. De
Coursey place, near Langford Bay)
BROWNE Edward 46 (d 1813 or 1815 in
his 6th yr)
BROWNE Edward 46 (b 1-7-1804; d
3-21-1857; aged 53 yrs, 2 mo., 14
days; wife: Julia A.)
BROWNE Julia A. 46 (d 9-18-1823, age
42 yrs)
BROWNE Louisa 46 (b 3-24-1810; d
9-22-1852)
BROWN'S Burial Ground (at Ringgold's
Fortune (see paragraph 53), once was
Brown's)
BRYAN family 69
BUDD family 91 (Two graves found in
1st row in cemetery at Clayton)
BULL Ann Webster 87 (b 12-26-1826; d
4-17-1912; m 9-21-1845 James Lamb
Bowers who d in Wilmington Del)
BULL Isaac 87
BULL Rebecca Reed 87 (b 12-26-1826; d
4-17-1912; m 9-21-1845 James Lamb
Bowers; d in Wilmington, Del)
BUTCHERS Neck 79 (farm owned in 1971
by Mrs. Jessie Jarrell)

CACY Anna Cephelia 39 (b 11-6-1845; d
Mar 25-1849; dau of John E. & Anna
Maria Osborne)

CACY Anna Maria Osborne 39 (b
12-11-1814; d 7-25-1880; wife of John
Evans Cacy
CACY Charles Osborne 39 (b 5-9-1850; d
9-21-1919; son of above)
CACY Elizabeth A. 39 (b 1809; d
10-2-1888, in her 79th year)
CACY John Evans 39 (b 1-27-1810; d
3-1-1860; wife: Anna Maria Osborne)
CACY John Evans 39 (b 11-1-1850; d
2-18-1851; son of Wm. T. & Mollie
Cacy)
CACY John Evans, Jr. 39 (b 8-25-1842;
d 11-6-1845; son of John Evans & Anna
M. Cacy)
CACY Marcia S. 39
CACY Mary Osborne 39 (b 3-2-1840; d
12-21-1912; wife of Wm. Evans Cacy)
CACY Mollie 39
CACY Stephen B. 39 (b 5-21-1868; d
6-3-1868; age 1 mo., 9 days)
CACY Stephen P. 39 (b 1833; d
4-13-1851; age 18 yrs 3 mo. 18 days)
CACY W. Finley Collins 39
CACY William 39 (b 9-14-1812; d
1-27-1892; wife: Elizabeth A.)
CACY William E. 39 (b 5-10-1888; d
4-22-1925)
CACY William Evans 39 (b 6-19-1906; d
8-6-1907)
CACY William T. 39
CAMP Mrs. Emory 59 (5 fieldstones in
old burial ground on her farm near
Galena)
CARRINGTON Raymond 70 (1970's owns
"Lamb's Meadows)
CAULK'S Field 20, 30 (War of 1812
battle site in Kent Co)
CECIL Friend's Meeting House 87
(Memorial Plaque & burial ground)
CEDAR Hill 57 (once owned by George
Lamb Bowers)
CHAPMAN --- 84 (Some stones left in
1971 at corner of Maryland Route 298
and Lynch Road)
CHAPMAN James W. 84 (wife: Mary Amanda
Webb)
CHAPMAN Mary Amanda Webb 84 (b
10-19-1837; d 4-28-1886)
CLARK'S Convenicney 13 (Norman Grieb
farm)

CLARK Denes 13 (7 fieldstone markers)
CLAYTON Cemetery 91
CLAYTON Jacob 91 (circa 1789;
gr-grandfather of William Clayton who
was 81 in 1971)
CLAYTON William 91
CLAYTON William C. 91
CLOTHIER Samuel 52 (b 1771; d
1-9-1832, age 61)
COCHE James, M.D. 50 (Friend of
Benjamin Comegys)
COCHRAN John 2
COLE Hynson E. 74
COLE Vernon 51 (Owner of Angelica
Nursery 1971 near Chesterville, Md.)
COLEMAN George 56 (b 1839; d
1-15-1867, aged 28 yrs)
COLLINS W. Finley 39 (10-27-1863; d
12-11-1918)
COMEGYS BIGHT farm 5
COMEGYS Ann 50 (b 1818; d 3-6-1831,
age 13; dau of John M. & Anna W.
Comegys)
COMEGYS Anna W. 50
COMEGYS Anne Cosden 63 (wife of Wm.
Comegys)
COMEGYS Benjamin 50 (b 1762; d
6-15-1809 at sea in his 47th yr)
COMEGYS 63 Cornelius (b 10-1780;
3-31-1815; Lieut. U.S.A., aged 34 yrs,
5 mo. Only son of Jesse & Mary
Comegys)
COMEGYS Edward 5 (b 4-12-1788; d
3-26-1865)
COMEGYS Farm 50 (between Chesterville
& Black's Station)
COMEGYS Hannah 50 (wife of Nathaniel
Comegys)
COMEGYS Hannah 50 (b 1-26-1775; d
12-28-1791; m 1-6-1791 Benjamin
Comegys; she was dau of Nathaniel &
Hannah Comegys)
COMEGYS Jesse 63 (b 10-30-1749; d
1---1804; son of Wm. & Anne Cosden
Comegys; wife: Mary Everett. A
soldier of the Revolution.)
COMEGYS John M. 50
COMEGYS Maria 50 (b 1840; d 4-20-1843,
age 3 yrs, 2 mo., 9 days; dau of John
& Anna W. Comegys)

GORDON Caroline A. 30 (b 1843; d
2-22-1845, age 1 yr, 6 mo., Stephney
Farm)
GORDON Charles 30 (m Elizabeth
Nicholson)
GORDON Dr. Joseph Nicholson 30
GORDON Elizabeth Nicholson 30 (dau of
Col. Joseph Nicholson)
GORDON James Frisby 30 (sold Stephney
farm in 1858)
GORDON Dr. Joseph Nicholson 30 (b
1775; d 4-28-1848, age 73 yrs; son of
Charles & Elizabeth Nicholson Gordon;
wife: Mary Frisby of Fairlee)
GORDON Mary Frisby 30
GRAHAM family 80
GRANGER 104 (date 1838; slave cemetery
on Blackiston farm)
GRANT burying ground 110 (Skinner's
Neck)
GRANT family 81
GRANT Mary E. 81 (d 1825; consort of
Richard E. Grant)
GRANT Richard E. 81
GRAYS Inn Point Farm 80 (home of Edgar
Strong in 1971)
GREENWOOD Cemetery 94
GREENWOOD Hannah 94 (d7-18-1866; wife
of Joseph Greenwood)
GREENWOOD Joseph 94
GRESHAM 66,80 (family burials at
Gray's Inn Point & at David Bramble
property)
GRIEB Norman 13
GRIFFITH Farm 99
GROVES James Henry 9 (b 6-10-1894; d
8-13-1977; in 1958 he & L. Wethered
Barroll moved Blay memorial stone
plaque to Shrewsbury Church; son of
James H. & Sally Rebecca Lamb Groves)
GUSTAFSON Elmer 27

HACKETT Anna Mary 74
HACKETT Charles 74
HACKETT Charles R. 74
HACKETT Henry 74
HACKETT Margaret J. 74
HACKETT Sibbella 74
HADDAWAY Ann 88
HADDAWAY Chapel 88

HADDAWAY Edward 88 (b 4-10-1830; d
10-10-1854, age 24 yrs, 6 mo.; son of
Edward & Ann Haddaway)
HADDAWAY John W. 88 (b 3-8-1835; d
12-10-1874)
HADDAWAY Joseph B. 88 (b 1874; d Nov
1878; son of Joseph B. & Mary E.
Haddaway)
HADDAWAY Mary E. 88 (wife of Joseph B.
Sr.)
HADDAWAY Richard 88 (b 6-22-1841; d
3-21-1865; age 23 yrs, 9 mo.; son of
Edward & Ann Haddaway)
HADDAWAY Tommy 89
HADDAWAY'S store 84
HALL Francis G. 24 (wife: Sarah
Tilghman Hall)
HALL Mary 24
HALL Sarah Tilghman 24 (b 3-28-1788; d
9-29-1812; dau of Matthew & Sarah
Tilghman)
HAMILTON Joshua Thomas 14 (d
9-26-1857, age 4 mo., 20 days; son of
Thomas D. & Sarah Hamilton)
HAMILTON Sarah 14 (b 1797; d 8-4-1870,
in her 73rd yr; wife of Thomas D.
Hamilton)
HAMILTON Susannah 14 (d 5-30-1841, age
7 yrs)
HAMILTON Thomas B. 14
HAMILTON Thomas D. 14 (d 3-20-1857, in
his 56th yr)
HANSON Jane E. 47 (b 7-1-1809; d
2-7-1883; m Dr. Thomas C. Kennard)
HANSON John 47 (b 1812; d 7-4-1826,
age 14 yrs; at Davis farm)
HARMAN Godfrey 69
HAROLD HILL farm 108
HARRIS Maria 75 (b 1775; d 7-3-1817,
age 42 yrs, 7 mo.; wife of Wm. Harris;
dau of Dr. James A. Anderson)
HARRIS William 75 (wife: Maria
Anderson)
HATCHERSON Farm 102
HATCHERSON Nancy 5
HATCHERSON Nathan 5
HAYES Farm 48 (once owned by John
Carville Sutton; Kennard burials - no
stones)
HAZEL Benjamin 74 (wife: Tempy Ann
Liza)

ANNOTATED INDEX (to paragraph numbers)

MAGGINNIS William C. 74
MAGINNIS Agnes 74 (b 1811; d
5-23-1812, age 1 yr, 4 mo. 23 days;
dau of Wm. & Mary Meginnis)
MAGINNIS Edwinn 74 (b 1848; d
2-18-1850; son of Wm. Maginnis)
MAGINNIS Margaret 74 (wife of William
C. Maginnis)
MAGINNIS Mary 74
MAGINNIS William C. 74 (b 5-28-1821; d
5-25-1881)
MAGINNIS Willie G. 74 (b 9-21-1846; d
2-22-1847, age 5 mo., 1 day)
MANN Thomas I. 51 (b 1850+; d
9-15-1852, in his 53rd yr; at Angelica
Nursery near Chesterville)
MANSFIELD Anna M. 75 (b 1790; d
1-31-1841, age about 50; wife of
Samuel Mansfield)
MANSFIELD Edmond 75 (wife: Mary I.;
Hynson Chapel)
MANSFIELD Mary I. 75 (wife of Edmond
Mansfield)
MANSFIELD Mary Ida 75 (b 9-27-1852; d
3-8-1854; dau of Edmond & Mary I.
Mansfield)
MANSFIELD Samuel 75 (b 1801; d
1-31-1837; footstone)
MARSH POINT 69
MASLIN burial ground 106 (Back of Mrs.
Julia Skirven's at Rock Hall)
MASLIN Anna Eliza Baker 23 (b
12-12-1799; d 5-5-1862; wife of Edwin
World Maslin; Langcroft Farm)
MASLIN Caroline 23 (m 9-13-1842 Robert
Ewing)
MASLIN Edwin World 23
MASLIN Elizabeth Blackiston 23
MASLIN Elizabeth Sarah Moieler 23 (m
Michael Miller Maslin)
MASLIN family 106
MASLIN Francis 23
MASLIN Hannah 23
MASLIN Jacob 23 (b 1784; d 12-31-1853;
m 12-18-1816 Rosamond Lamb; she d 22
days later)
MASLIN James 23
MASLIN John A. 23
MASLIN Lawrence D. 88 (b 1860; d
5-30-1862, age 2 yrs, 4 mo.)
MASLIN Martha Glenn 23

MASLIN Mary Ann Lamb 23 (b 9-8-1714; d
3-8-1748; dau of Francis & Rosamond
Beck Lamb; m 12-11-1735 Thomas Maslin
II, his 1st wife)
MASLIN Michael Miller 23 (b 1778; d
2-8-1852; m Elizabeth S. Moieler at
York Pa)
MASLIN Nettie M. 88 (b 2-9-1858; d
6-9-1862, age 4 yrs, 4 mo.)
MASLIN Rebecca Thomas Ferrill 23
MASLIN Rosamond 23 (b 8-10-1789; d
1-22-1854; dau of George & Sarah
Briscoe Lamb; m 12-18-1816 Jacob
Maslin)
MASLIN Susan J. 23 (b 1837; d
5-17-1863, age 26 yrs)
MASLIN Susan Jemima 23 (b 1838; dau of
John A. & Elizabeth Blackiston Maslin)
MASLIN Thomas II 23
MASLIN Thomas I. 23
MASLIN Thomas III 23
MASSEY Charles A. 40 (b 1833; d
9-24-1835; son of E. E. & M. E.
Massey)
MASSEY Charles F. 40 (b 1841; d
5-11-1843; son of E. E. & M. E.
Massey)
MASSEY Col. Elijah E. 40 (b 7-3-1814;
d 1-23-1881, age 66 yrs, 6 mo., 20
days; wife: Mary E.)
MASSEY Eleanora P. 40 (b 1843; d
8-24-1845); dau of E. E. & M. E.
Massey)
MASSEY Henrietta A. 40 (b 1845; d
4-19-1853, in her 8th yr; dau of E. E.
& M. E. Massey)
MASSEY Mary E. 40 (b 1805; d
1-29-1859, in her 44th yr; wife of
Elijah E. Massey)
MASSEY Mary E. 40 (b 1845; d
9-17-1864, in her 19th yr; dau of E.
E. & M. E. Massey)
MASSEY Robert H. 40 (b 9-23-1859; d
12-25-1876, age 17 yrs, 5 mo., 27
days)
Massey Thomas J. 40 (b 1840; d
9-4-1843, age 3 yrs)
McCLAREY (McCleary) Mrs. 79 (bur c.
1879 on Butchers Neck)

McGINNIS George 100 (b 1786; d 12-29-1829, age 43 yrs, 1 mo., 18 days)
McGUIRE Benjamin 70 (1971 owner of Swarthmore on Route 298 near Kennedyville)
McHENRY Mr. 68
MEGINNIS B. 100 (b 2-26-1791; d 1-23-1815; on Munyon's farm)
MEGINNIS Infant 74 (d 5-22-1853; son of Wm. C. & Margaret Meginnis)
MELITOTA 72
MELVIN Ann R. Bowers 87 (b 8-8-1848; d 1-16-1882; dau of James L. & Rebecca B. Bowers; m 5-12-1867 Thomas W. Melvin)
MELVIN Rosamond 87 (b 12-23-1867; d 9-3-1871; dau of Thomas W. & Ann R. Bowers Melvin)
MELVIN Thomas W. 87
MEREDITH 76 (maker of grave marker)
MERRITT Ann R. 5 (b 2-12-1812; d 10-26-1857; at Comegys Bight farm)
MIDDLETON John P. Sr. 64 (b 1853; d 1934; Ashley burial ground)
MIDDLETON Mary Ellen 64 (b 2-24-1862; d 12-17-1911; Ashley burial ground; wife of John P. Middleton Sr.)
MIDDLETON Phoebe G. 64 (b 12-9-1856; d 5-14-1883; wife of John P. Middleton; dau of David C. & Mary Ashley)
MIER Leonard 44
MILLARD Joiner farm 72
MILLER Irving Tillnian 97 (Spring Grove burying ground)
MILLER Burying Ground 97

MILLINGTON Friend's Burial Ground 41 (Millington Md.)
MINTA 22 (b 1770; d 11-15-1836; inscription: "Faithful & valiant servant of the Bordley family." E. Lloyd photo)
MIDDLETON Phoebe G. 64 (b 12-9-1856; d 5-14-1883; wife of John P. Middleton; dau of David C. & Mary Ashley)
MIER Leonard 44
MILLARD Joiner farm 72
MILLER Irving Tillnian 97 (Spring Grove burying ground)
MILLER Burying Ground 97

MILLINGTON Friend's Burial Ground 41 (Millington Md.)
MINTA 22 (b 1770; d 11-15-1836; inscription: "Faithful & valiant servant of the Bordley family." E. Lloyd photo)
MOFFETT Cemetery 49 (on Moffett farm)
MOFFETT Elizabeth P. 49 (b 1739; d 1-1-1775, age 36; wife of George Moffett)
MOFFETT Farm 62 (owned in 1971 by Mrs. Julia Nicholson Jervis)
MOFFETT G. Robert Sr. 29
MOFFETT George 49 (wife: Elizabeth)
MOFFETT William 104 (1971 owner of Blackiston place, between Massey & Millington)
MOIELER Elizabeth Sarah 23
MONEY Eliza R. 74 (b 3-19-1822; d 3-30-1865; wife of Joseph N. Money, age 43 yrs, 11 days)
MONEY Joseph N. 74 (b 1790; d 9-23-1828, in his 38th yr)
MONEY R. 74
MORRIS family 90 (family burials on old Morris farm near Golt)
MORRIS Farm 90
MUNYON Mr. 100
MURPHY Elizabeth 52 (b 1770; d 5-10-1806; bur near Massey at old Episcopal Rectory site; age 36 yrs, 1 mo.)
MYERS Leonard 44 (Possum Hollow; unmarked vaults)
MYERS Milton 43 (1971 owner of part of Worton Manor; old Scone burial ground)

NAPLEY GREEN 54 (1975 - building on site of two old graves; no markers)
NEAL Edgar H. 40 (b 10---1868; d 9-13-1870, age 1 yr, 11 mo.)
NEAL Eliza L. 40
NEAL Willard C. 40 (b 5-17-1864; d 7-13-1864, age 2 mo., 26 days; son of W. H. and Eliza L. Neale)
NEALE Charles K. 40 (b 3-27-1862; d 4-20-1877; son of W. H. & E. L. Neale; on Hendrickson, now Anderson, farm)
NEALE E. L. 40
NEALE W. H. 40

2-18-1824 Rachel Atkinson; m(2)
12-10-1832 Mary R. Bowers)
PARROTT Benjamin William Bowers 87 (b
9-11-1835; d 10-13-1856; son of
Benjamin & Mary R. Bowers Parrott)
PARROTT Elma Bowers Hopkins 87 (b
11-25-1843; d 4-29-1930; wife of
George Richard Parrott; they had 8
children, none married)
PARROTT Emily May 87 (b 10-8-1872; d
3-22-1929; dau of above)
PARROTT George Elwood 87 (b 2-24-1869;
d 7-19-1926; son of above)
PARROTT George Richard 87 (b 3-1-1838;
d 8-26-1898; son of Benjamin & Mary R.
Bowers Parrott; m Elma Bowers Hopkins)
PARROTT Harrie Wilson 87 (b 7-31-1882;
d 8-19-1882; son of above)
PARROTT Howard H. 87 (b 12-31-1877; d
8-21-1903; son of above)
PARROTT John Ellwood 87 (b 8-7-1867; d
11-7-1868; son of George Richard &
Elma Bowers Hopkins Parrott)
PARROTT Lillie Bowers 87 (b 12-8-1875;
d 12-31-1938; dau of above)
PARROTT Mary Rebecca Bowers 87 (b
8-5-1816; d 9-9-1887; m(1) 12-10-1832
Benjamin Parrott; m(2) Joseph Usilton)
PARROTT Rachel 87
PARROTT Robert Thomas 87 (b 7-31-1844;
d 8-31-1851; son of above)
PARROTT Sarah Lamb 87 (b 10-27-1833; d
9-1-1887; dau of above; m 12-16-1864
Charles W. Warren)
PARROTT Willie Benjamin 87 (b
11-4-1870; d 11-23-1870; son of George
R. & Elma Bowers Hopkins Parrott)
PARSONS Harrison, Isaac, John, Lewis
71 (early owners of Baxter (1971)
place on Smithville Road; once was a
Parsons burial ground in the field
near the corner)
PEACOCK John 50 (1971 owner of Comegys
farm near Crumpton; one fieldstone)
PEACOCK Joseph 50 (1971 owner of
Comegys farm between Chesterville and
Black's Station)
PEARCE Anna 19 (Colchester farm, near
Galena; listed on monument dated 1847)
PEARCE Aquilla 9 (incorrectly named as
2nd husband of Rachel Blay on plaque

on front of Shrewsbury Church; it
should read Aquila Paca)
PEARCE Colonel 9
PEARCE Edward 86 (b 11-20-1808; d
8-1-1809; son of G. & J. Pearce)
PEARCE Elizabeth 19 (on monument at
Colchester)
PEARCE Gideon 86 (wife: Juliana
Woodland)
PEARCE Isabella 19 (monument at
Colchester farm)
PEARCE James 19 (monument at
Colchester farm)
PEARCE Mr. and Mrs. 19 (monument at
Colchester farm)
PEARCE Mrs. Julia 19 (monument at
Colchester farm)
PEARCE Juliana Woodland 86 (b
3-14-1788; d 2-8-1809; dau of John &
Mary Woodland; wife of Gideon Pearce;
bur at Spry Landing)
PEARCE Martha 9
PEARCE Rachel 9
PEARCE Rebekah 37 (b 6-21-1792; d
11-24-1834; m 1-18-1818 Wm. Lamb of
Fair Hope, Kent Co)
PEARCE William 69
PENNELL Harry 87 (b 6-27-1868; d
8-8-1868; son of Samuel & Noll
Pennell)
PENNELL Mary J. B. 87 (age 13 yrs, 2
mo.; dau of above)
PENNELL Noll 87 (wife of Samuel
Pennell)
PENNELL Robert 87 (b 9-5-1854; d
11-15-1872; son of above)
PENNELL Sallie J. 87 (b 11-1-1860; d
11-16-1869; dau of Samuel & Noll
Pennell)
PENNELL Samuel M. 87 (wife: Noll
Pennell)
PENNINGTON Susan A. 17 (b 3-5-1845; d
8-30-1908; dau of Cornelius & Emmeline
Silcox Pennington of Delaware; m
1-13-1864 John Henry Jarvis)
PERKINS Anna 12 (b 1794; d 6-9-1861,
in her 67th yr; dau of Daniel &
Susannah Perkins)
PERKINS Caroline 12 (b 10-28-1804; d
6-22-1882; Brice's Mill)

RINGGOLD Rebecca 16 (b 1776; d
9-20-1857, in her 81st yr; wife of
Edward Ringgold)
RINGGOLD William 35 (wife: Mary
Ringgold)
RINGGOLD William Edward 16 (b
12-31-1843; d 2-1-1852)
RINGGOLD'S FORTUNE 53 (on Ricaud's
Branch & west fork of Langford creek;
1970's owner: Stefan Skipp)
ROGERS Meliscent 35 (d -8-1800; Old
Field Point)
ROGERS Richard Hynson 53
ROLLISON John E. 64 (b 1881; d 1947)
ROLLISON Mary E. 64 (b 1885; d 1957)
RUTH John C. 14 (father of infant b &
d 1847)
RUTH Sallie G. 14 (wife of John C.
Ruth)
RYLAND Edward R. 52 (b 12-14-1839; d
4-8-1880, age 40 yrs, 3 mo. 25 days)

SCHAEFFER Mrs. Charles 33
SCONE 68 Old name of farm near the
Presbyterian Church, Kennedyville)
SCONE Arthur A. 43 (d 1811; fieldstone
marked "A.S." at present Milton Myers
home, part of old Worton Manor)
SCONE Rachel K. 43 (b 1789; d
5-21-1815; consort of Arthur A. Scone)
SCONE William 78 (b 1793; d 3-3-1846,
aged 53)
SEWELL Eleanor 64 (wife of George
Sewell)
SEWELL Ellen Clyde 64 (b 11-8-1874; d
11-20-1879; dau of George & Eleanor
Sewell)
SEWELL George 64
SHEPPERD family 90 (family burials on
old Morris farm on Golt-Hurlock Cor.
Road)
SHRIVER James F. 64 (Co. B., 2 E. F.
Md. Inf.; Ashley Cemetery, Piney Neck)
SIMMONS Emoline 14 (wife of Wm.
Simmons; Providence Plantation)
SIMMONS Sarah E. 14 (b 6-13-1833; d
3-31-1912)
SIMMONS William 14 (husband of
Emoline)
SIMNS Jacquette farm 109

SKINNERS Neck 81 (1971 owner of farm –
Hodges Crouch)
SKIPP Stefen 53 (1975 owner of
Ringgold's Fortune)
SKIRVEN Julia 106
SMITH Hannah 16 (b 1779; d 6-21-1851,
in her 72nd yr; wife of William Smith)
SMITH William 16 (wife: Hannah)
SMYTH Margaret 24
SMYTH Sarah 24
SMYTH Thomas 24 (b 4-2-1723; d
3-19-1813, age 90 yrs, less 14 days)
SMYTHE family 103 (family burials at
Ratcliffe Cross)
SPEARS Edward W. 74 (wife: Mary J.
Spears)
SPEARS Mary J. 74 (b 5-25-1848; d
6-26-1870, age 22 yrs, 1 mo., 1 day)
SPRING COVE 97
SPRING HILL 98
SPRINKLE Mrs. Jane Brooks 93
SPRY Landing Farm 86 (owned in 1971 by
Ralph Bateman; on River Road, along
Chester River below Crumpton)
STARCK Benjamin 22
STARK Benjamin 22 (b 11-9-1814; d
1-18-1854; Andelot?)
STARK Capt. B. H. 42 (wife: Catherine
E. Stark; Knoll Farm)
STARK Catherine 22 (b 1748; d 1818;
Andelot – Timm's Creek)
STARK Catherine E. 42 (b 6-4-1809; d
5-27-1854; wife of Capt. B. H. Stark)
STARKEY Farms 35 (Old Field Point,
near Galena)
STAVELY family 34 (burials at Knock's
Folly)
STAVELY Mrs. Frances 3 (birthplace: 17
room brick house, part of Great Oak
Manor, owned then by her father)
STAVELY R. W. 84
STOKES Charles P. 37 (1971 owner of
Fair Hope Farm)
STOKES Mrs. C. P. 37 (d 1969)
STRONG --- 102 (family burials along
Baker's Lane North of Route 20 on farm
presently owned by Hatcherson)
STRONG Edgar 80
STRONG Robert 76
STUART Doc. A. 6

TURNER Elizabeth 87 (b 1826; d 1903)
TURNER Joseph 87 (b 1765; d 6-8-1841, age 76 yrs)
TURNER Martha E. 87 (b 12-28-1840; d 11-16-1911)
TURNER Rebecca 87 (b 1845; d 1908)
TURNER Richard B. 87 (b 1811; d 1900)
TURNER Richard T. 87 (b 1819; d 1892)
TURNER Sara 87 (d 6-8-1845)

USILTON Bob 89
USILTON Joseph (2nd husband of Mary Rebecca Bowers, dau of Wm. & Sarah Lamb Bowers; see paragraph 87)
USILTON Margaret E. 87
USILTON Mary Rebecca Bowers Parrott 87 (b 8-5-1816; d 9-9-1887; m(2) Joseph Usilton)
USILTON Robert 71

Van STOHL C. 21
VANSANT Ada D. 41 (wife of Andrew A. Vansant) Both this and the following entry show as parents of John Nicholas Vansant, b 12-24-1899, d 8-17-1901, apparently in error)
VANSANT Ada G. 41 (wife of Andrew W. Vansant) See above item.
VANSANT Ada M. 41 (b 4-8-1853; d 3-23-1879, age 25 yrs, 11 mo., 15 days; Millington Quaker Burial Ground)
VANSANT Andrew A. or W. 41 (wife: Ada A. or Ada G.)
VANSANT Emily A. 41 (b 12-13-1842; d 3-18-1911)
VANSANT Florence C. 41 (b 6-2-1808; d 9-22-1808, 3 mo, 20 days)
VANSANT Harry C. 41 (b 9-20-1880; d 5-29-1906; footstone: Brother)
VANSANT J. Margaret 41 (d April; marker too worn to read)
VANSANT John N. 41 (b 9-26-1840; d 5-16-1906)
VANSANT John Nicholas 41 (b 12-24-1899; d 8-17-1901; son of Andrew & Ada Vansant)
VANSANT Mary H. 41 (b 6-22-1817; d 12-18-1847)
VANSANT Nicholas A. 41 (b 11-6-1869; d 1-11-1871; son of John N. & Emily A. Vansant)

VANSANT Nicholas C. 41 (b 2-19-1872; d 4-24-1875; son of same)
VANSANT R. 41 (wife of Nicholas; has dau Ada M.
VAN STOLK C. 21 (of Rotterdam, Holland; owner of Caulk's Field Farm & Tulip Forest Farm off Route 20)
VANZANT Miss Helena 17 (granddaughter of John Henry & Susan A. Pennington Jarvis)
VICKERS Benjamin 26 (b 11-18-1761; d 5-29-1835; farm in Quaker Neck now owned by Henry W. Johnston)
VICKERS John E. 88 (b 1849; d 1908; Haddaway Chapel site)
VICKERS Sarah E. 88 (b 1854; d 1893; wife of John E. Vickers)
VOSHELL Hennella 74 (wife of John F. Voshell)
VOSHELL John F. 74
VOSHELL Mary F. 74 (d 6-21-1888, age 1 mo.; dau of above)
VOSHELL Sarah A. 74
VOSHELL Thomas H. 74
VOSHELL William T. 74

WALLERS Benjamin P. 41
WALLERS Emma L. 41 (d 9 mo. old; dau of above)
WALLIS Emily Thomas 63 (b 1803; d 3-2-1896, in her 93rd yr; wife of Francis L. Wallis)
WALLIS Francis L. 63 (b 1804; d 4-7-1855, in his 51st yr)
WALLIS Mary Emily 63 (b 1839; d 3-7-1841, age 18 mo., 2 days)
WALLIS William John 63 (b 3---1830; d 5-25-1831, age 14 mo.; son of Francis L. & Emily Wallis)
WARREN Charles W. 87 (b 11-4-1835; d 10-24-1885; m 12-16-1864 Sarah Lamp Parrott)
WARREN Mamie B. 87 (b 12-24-1865; d 2-27-1870; dau of Charles W. & Sarah Lamb Parrott Warren)
WARREN Sarah (Sally) Lamb Parrott 87 (b 10-27-1833; d 9-1-1887); m 12-16-1864 Charles W. Warren; dau of Benjamin & Mary Rebecca Bowers Parrott)
Washington Park 32

WATKINS Mary Helen 76 (b 1839; d
8-18-1854, age 15 yrs, 7 mo., 3 wks, 5
days; wife of Shadrach Watkins)
WATKINS Shadrach 76
WATSON Louise 5
WATTS Farm 45
WATTS Mildred 45 (granddaughter of
former owner of Watts farm; m Merritt
Fogwell)
WEBB family 34 (burials at Knock's
Folly)
WEBB Mary 84 (wife of William Webb)
WEBB Mary Amanda 84 (b 10-19-1837; d
4-28-1886; dau of Wm. & Mary Webb)
WEBB Virginia 34 (b 1842; d 10-8-1845,
age 3 yrs, 2 mo.; at Knock's Folly)
WEBB William 84 (wife: Mary)
WEBB William 89 (b 1840; d 12---1861,
age 21 yrs, 1 mo.; near corner of
Route 298 at Lynch
WEBB William D. 34 (b 1840; d
8-18-1844, aged 4; at Knock's Folly)
WESTCOTT Mrs. Simon 33 (1970 owner of
Glen More Farm)
WETHERED Issabella Tilden 9 (wife of
Richard Wethered)
WETHERED John 9 (1st John, 2nd son of
Richard & Isaballa Tilden Wethered)
WETHERED John 9 (2nd John, 4th son of
Richard & Isaballa Tilden Wethered; d
2-21-1822, in his 77th yr)
WETHERED Richard 9 (wife: Isabella
Tilden)
WETHERED Samuel 9 (3rd son of Richard
& Isabella Tilden Wethered)
WETHERED William 9 (1st son of above)
All these Wethereds are listed on the
plaque taken from Blay's Range to
Shrewsbury Church in 1958.
WHITELAW farm 42
WHITELAW William 42 (1970's owner of
Knoll Farm)
WICKES 108 family burials on Harold
Hill's farm below Edesville. 2 marble
stones.
WICKES Anna Maria 1 (b 1826; d
4-2-1864, aged 38 yrs)
WICKES B. Chambers 1 (b 1823; d
7-1-1854, in his 31st yr)

WICKES Burying ground 108 (on Harold
Hill's farm below Edesville; 2 marble
stones)
WICKES Colonel Joseph 1
WICKES Elizabeth 12 (b 1772; d
5---1850, aged 78)
WICKES Elizabeth C. 1 (b 1799; d
3-10-1872, aged 73 yrs)
WICKES Ezekiel Chambers 1 (b 1831; d
6-30-1861, in his 30th yr)
WICKES Joseph 1 (b 1759; d 8-16-1822,
age 63)
WICKES Col. Joseph 1 (b 9-2-1788; d
1-14-1864)
WICKES Joseph N. 1
WICKES Mary 1 (b 1764; d 3-29-1823,
age 59)
WICKES Sarah 1 (b 1786; d 8-26-1844,
age 58)
The above Wickes family members are
buried on the farm owned in the 1970's
by Wilbur Ross Hubbard, once the
Wickes home.
WILKENS Edward 13 (b 1769; d 5-5-1814,
in his 45th yr, bur at Clark's
Conveniency)
WILKINS James T. 14 (b 2-10-1810; d
4-16-1882; bur at Providence
Plantation, Quaker Neck)
WILLIAMS family 60 (once owned a farm
called Rich Levels; 1978 owner: Olin
Davis; near Golt)
WILLOWFIELDS 70 (older name of
Swarthmore, now called Sycamore Farm)
WILLSON Anna M. 24 (b 1806; d
4-28-1823; wife of Tho. Willson, age
37; at Trumpington, Eastern Neck)
WILLSON D. C. 24 (b 10-21-1828; d
3-5-1876; footstone: D. C. W.
WILLSON Ernest 24 (1970's -
Trumpington Farm; m Miss Mary
Ringgold)
WILLSON family 77 (Family burials on
Aiello Farm, Eastern Neck, where the
daffodil field was in the 1970's)
WILLSON Mary A. 24 (b 1815; d
6-4-1847, aged 32; wife of Tho.
Wilson)
WILLSON Thomas 24 (b 9-28-1778; d
10-28-1859; son of Thomas S. B. & Mary
Hall Willson)

ANNOTATED INDEX (to paragraph numbers)

WILLSON Thomas S. B. 24
WILMER Ann 30
WILMER family 92 (family burials on
farm owned in 1970's by Mrs. Ann
Wilmer Hoon)
WILMER Farm 92
WILMER Lemual 30 (sold Stephney Manoi
in July 1822
WILMER Phil 92
WILMER William 30
WILSON Anna 35 (wife of George Wm.
Wilson; Old Field Point)
WILSON Anna M. 24
WILSON Anna Williamina 35 (b 1821; d
8-31-1841; dau of George W. & Anna
Wilson)
WILSON D. C. 24
WILSON Edwin 35 (b 1814; d 8-5-1814,
age 7 mo., 21 days; son of Robert &
Eliza Wilson)
WILSON Eliza 35 (wife of Robert)
WILSON George William 35 (b 1783; d
12-30-1841; wife Anna Wilson)
WILSON Margaret 35 (9-4-1812; d
9-17-1813, age 1 yr, 13 days)
WILSON Mary 35 (wife of Robert)
WILSON Robert 35 (wife: Eliza)
WILSON Robert 35 (b 9-1-1815; d
11-4-1816; son of Robert & Eliza
Wilson)
WILSON Robert 35 (wife: Mary; son d
1822
WILSON Thomas 24
WILSON Wilbert 35 (b 2-6-1822; d
5-28-1822; son of Robert & Mary
Wilson)
WILSON William George 35 (b 5-11-1817;
d 12-16-1845, age 28 yrs, 7 mo. 5 da)
WINTERNIGHT H. 46 (Baltimore monument
maker)
WOODLAND John 86 (Spry Landing)
WOODLAND Juliana 86 (b 3-14-1788; d
2-8-1809; dau of John & Mary Woodland;
m Gideon Pearce)
WOODLAND Mary 86 (wife of John
Woodland)
WORTON 67
WORTON Manor 43
WORTON William 64 (b 8-22-1803; d
10-30-1850; Ashley burial ground,
Piney Neck)

WROTH Dr. P. 10 (See Peregrine below)
WROTH Edward T. 10 (wife: Eugenia
Maria (Wroth) Wroth; Mary Morris Road)
WROTH Eugenia Marie 10 (b 2-26-1817; d
9-30-1861; dau of Peregrine & Martha
P. Wroth; wife of Edward T. Wroth)
WROTH Margaret S. Nicols 10 (b
3-31-1802; d 12-13-1836; m 6-19-1827
Dr. P. Wroth; dau of Samuel & Eliza
Nichols)
WROTH Martha P. 10 (b 8-5-1779; d
9-23-1826; m 8-27-1807 Dr. P. Wroth;
dau of John & Milcah Page)
WROTH Mary Cecilia 10 (b 7-10-1808; d
7-30-1808, age 20 days)
WROTH Peregrine, M. D. 10 (b
4-7-1786; d 6-13-1879, age 93; m(1)
Martha Page; m(2) Margaret S. Nichols)

YOATES ---- 102 (grave found on
Hatcherson Farm)
YOATES ---- 105 (grave found at Goose
Hill Farm, owned by Clayton Hicks in
1970's)

-49-